KERRI POMAROLLI

MOMS' NIGHT OUT

and other things i miss...

DEVOTIONS TO HELP YOU SURVIVE!

B&H
PUBLISHING GROUP
Nashville, Tennessee

ISBN: 978-1-4336-8484-5

B&H Publishing Group
Nashville, Tennessee

Dewey Decimal Classification: 242.643

Subject Heading: MOTHERS \ DEVOTIONAL
LITERATURE \ FAMILY LIFE

Representation by WTA Services, LLC,
Smyrna, TN.

Unless otherwise noted, Scripture quotations are taken from
the Holman Christian Standard Bible®, Copyright © 1999,
2000, 2002, 2003, 2009 by Holman Bible Publishers.

Also used: English Standard Version (ESV), copyright © 2001
by Crossway Bibles, a publishing ministry of Good News
Publishers. ESV Text Edition: 2007. All rights reserved.

Also used: New International Version (NIV), copyright ©
1973, 1978, 1984, 2011 by International Bible Society.

Also used: Contemporary English Version (CEV), © American
Bible Society 1991, 1992, used by permission.

To see more comedy, and to read more from Wendy Hagen
and Kristin Weber, please go to www.wendyhagen.net and
kristinweberonline.com.

2 3 4 5 6   17 16 15 14

Dedication

I was going to dedicate this to my loving family but instead I dedicate it to my super agent Bill Reeves.

He had a lot more to do with this book being written than they did. Here's to the tortoise and the hare!

Acknowledgment

Many thanks to Dawn Woods, my wonderful editor; Bill and Barry, my super agents; Amelia, my left brain; my mighty Women Prayer Warriors; my Mommy Mafia Bunco Ladies; the makers of Nutella; "The Woman" and my Wednesday Night Rowdy Group; my Friday Night Willie Wonka Crew; my Facebook posse; LaTanya, Tina, Debbie, Kim H., Shari, Uncle Scott, Julie T., Gia, Auntie Nee Nee, and Gayle (in Dallas)—my best cheerleaders.

To Wendy Hagen, Kristin Weber, and Claire Lee for their hilarious contributions.

Thanks to my "Well Family" and my SOS team; my Cho and Chung Family, who inspire great comedy, as well as my partner in the Momland, Angela Hoover.

Thanks to everyone who inspired the events of this book, not excluding ex-boyfriends, Pinterest, and celebrity moms that I'm jealous of.

Acknowledgments

Thanks to my brother Mark, the best uncle in the world. Thanks to Barb for being the kind of mom you write books about in the best way possible. Thanks to Dad for being my biggest PR rep in public. I love you.

To my daughter Lucy, you brought comedy relief to this book and every day of my life. You amuse me with your wit and amaze me with your faith. To Ruby, you bring joy to my world and inspire miracles all around you. To Ron, you used to make me tea, but now you're too busy giving our kids baths because you know I hate it. That's love! Thanks for doing all that stuff I never thank you for!

God, thank You for giving me kids so I can record all the things they've put me through and have evidence in their adulthood. Thank You Lord for "Team McGehee!"

Contents

Contents

Introduction

When I was asked to write this book, I thought to myself, *No way*! I don't have time to write a book because I'm too busy trying to escape Costco without buying lawn furniture and a TV, convincing my six-year-old that she can't start dating, selling cookie dough for my preschooler's fundraiser, and selling wrapping paper for my kindergartener's fundraiser so she doesn't get left out of the Chuck E Cheese Pizza party for the "winners"!

Ahhh, the joys of motherhood! Who knew? There wasn't a manual on raising kids without committing a felony. My husband reminded me you need a permit to buy a cat and a license to rent a golf cart, but anyone can become a parent. As I'm writing this, my daughter is doing shots with those tiny yogurt drinks behind my back because she thinks I can't see her through the back of my head. Should I be mad? Well, it is yogurt after all and there's some calcium there. Last time something like this happened she was three and overdosed on Flintstone gummy vitamins. We found her under the table like an addict about to be shipped off to rehab.

When I took on this task, I thought to myself I'd love to write this inspiring devotional for all those super spiritual put together Pinterest moms out there with their home-made organic home-schooled cotton candy machines that carve Scripture verses and their Tupperware with matching lids! I love you guys! I want to be you guys!

But, where are the moms who are serving their toddlers Tic Tacs from the bottom of their purse because they forgot to pack snacks for the "play date," which they are forty-five minutes late for? Where are the moms who can't remember the last time they shaved *both* legs in the shower? Is this you? Read on. By the way, Pinterest Moms, you can read on too and correct my grammar. Also, I'm planning a puppy birthday party and I need decor ideas!

I love God with all my heart even on the days when I feel like there is nothing left of it. I love God when I am, as David said in the Bible, "In the slimy pit!" (of spaghetti). I need God most during this "so called season" of motherhood. They say the madness will pass and someday all the socks in my laundry will have mates. Someday I won't feel so "dirty" all the time from the constant trail of grime that follows me wherever I go, but somehow I'm supposed to enjoy it. I'm supposed to "savor" these moments. I'm trying, I really am. I think God loves it when I'm frazzled and crazy because it's in those times I can hear Him. To me, I'm sure God is laughing along with me at my life, comforting me to fight on through another day. I want to write this devotional for those of us that are living the "Real Life." Not the kind of devotional that is written about achieving perfection. Put the magazines down ladies! They are from the Devil! Angelina Jolie has one nanny for each individual kid.

I'm doing my best to live this life He's given me through tear stains, lost tap shoes, and late night cuddles. I know one thing for sure. I don't want to miss any of it. I know it's truly by the grace of God that my entire family and I have survived this long. I know it's my constant struggle to "go deeper" with God. I buy books, read devotionals, and watch teachings of women who seem to have "the answer." I downloaded the Bible app on my cell phone, but I realized you actually have to use it for it to do any good. I'm too busy checking my Facebook status to see how many people like my new haircut. I think I'm done with all of that for now. I'm not going to beat myself up for not being spiritual enough or "deep enough" with my Father God. I think what He's telling me is to slow down and realize that I, Kerri Pomarolli, am exactly enough as I am. Are you with me? Good! Wait, my six-year-old is laid out in the kitchen with twelve bottles of mini-yogurt drinks surrounding her. I'll be right back. "Hello, Poison Control? Yeah . . . it's me, Kerri again!"

You Can't Quit Birth

"Before she goes into labor, she gives birth; before the pains come upon her, she delivers a son." ~ Isaiah 66:7 *(NIV)*

When I was pregnant with my first child, I naively knew one thing . . . I was *not* going to have a C-Section. I had this prayer book about *Super Natural Birth* filled with stories of fifteen minute labors and women who prayed themselves through seamless deliveries. I just knew that would be me.

When my water broke, I bopped into the hospital with my cute little birth plan—NO C-SECTION. Well, thirty-six hours later I was only dilated to a one and my doctor said, "Look, we have to get this baby out and a C-Section is the only option." At that point, I just looked at my husband, during a contraction, and said, "Pack my bags, we're leaving. I'm not having surgery. I *quit*." My honorary doula/friend Cathy smiled lovingly and said, "Kerri, you can't quit birth. One way or another you *are* going to give birth to this baby. We've prayed and God must have a plan that is best, and you have to trust Him right now. You're almost there. You have to keep going!" It didn't seem like I was almost anywhere. I had been in labor for thirty-six hours and had nothing to show for it. Dilated to a one? What a failure. I could beat myself up. But when labor isn't going according to plan, no one blames the mother because it's not her fault.

Thirty minutes later on that Tuesday night in October, I gave birth to a beautiful 10 pound, 6 ounce butterball! You heard me! The doctor looked at her and said, "Don't breastfeed her . . . get her a pizza!" She was so big, she drove home!

After becoming a mom, I became a prayer warrior for my kids. There's a situation I've been battling for one of my daughters and I haven't seen it fully come into fruition yet, but God made me a promise that it WILL happen. When God makes a promise and you don't see it, there is a birthing process that you sometimes need to go through, and it can be quite painful. But just like labor, even if there are complications, you don't quit . . . you keep pushing and pushing and pushing . . . until you see what you're praying for.

Whatever you're fighting for, don't quit. Whatever you are "birthing"—a healing, a restored marriage, a child— keep fighting. Just PUSH:

P—Proclaim God's promises. Say them out loud and feel yourself getting stronger.

U—Understand your authority. God has given us authority over all the schemes of the Devil. Exercise it and the Devil must flee.

S—Stand on the Word. Find a verse that fits what you are fighting for (healing, provision, restoration). When the Devil attacks you with doubt, pull out the promise in God's Word and stand on it!

H—Help others in the process before and after your miracle has arrived. This is warfare in and of itself. You're letting the enemy know you're not backing down and you are dangerous.

Once you've agreed to stand with God and His promises for your life, there is *no going back*. There is no way it's *not* going to happen. The Devil will try to lie to you . . . he will be crafty and give you thirty-six hours of labor and then a C-Section, but in the end of it I got my double portion. I got a 10 pound, 6 ounce baby!

I got more than I ever expected and God knew it needed to be a C-Section so I could still walk today. He knew the battle I had to fight. He knew the promise I was carrying in my womb until it was time to let it out and see it with my own eyes. I chose to believe there was a promise as big as a mustard seed inside of me and I nurtured it and fed it and sang to it and nine months later she came. And then all the pain was forgotten. God wiped it away. He wiped it away so much I did it all again.

Now that you know you can't quit, how can you and God work together to bring His promises into your life?

Take a MOMENT to think about . . .

1. What promises are you praying for? What burdens do you carry?
2. What Scripture can you reference to help you with your burdens?

Lord, I stand on Your promises in my life. I rebuke doubt and fear and believe that what You say is true. I will not quit "pushing" for all that You have for me and my family. Amen.

Disney Princesses Make Me Cry

"Love bears all things, believes all things, hopes all things, endures all things." ~ 1 Corinthians 13:7 (ESV)

It never used to be this way. I'd watch Cinderella and Snow White ride off into the sunset with their handsome prince and never shed a tear. But lately, as a mom, some of these movies are different for me.

It started with the movie *Brave*. It was the first time I took both of my daughters to a movie together. Ruby was only two, but she was groovin' with the 3D glasses and the popcorn. At the end of the film, there is the scene where the mama bear almost sacrifices her life for her daughter. It was gut-wrenching and I was bawling while tightly holding my five-year-old in my arms. Lucy was like "Mom, why are you crying? It was her daughter that turned her into a bear in the first place. I don't get it." I sobbed all the way home saying, "You will honey, you will!" Maybe I was PMSing that day.

It also happened when I took the girls to see *Frozen*, the newest Disney offering in the fairy tale genre, which is about two sisters and their battle to break the curse that one of the sister's has had since birth in which everything she touches turns to ice. We sang along and rooted for the heroine as she trekked across snow and mountains to find her sister who was voluntarily in hiding because she didn't want to hurt anyone. Yes, there were princes involved. To break the spell there had to be a true act of love, and everyone was assuming it was going to be a kiss from Prince Charming. Well, Prince Charming wasn't so charming after all and as it turned out, he was trying to steal the royal throne. The true act of love that broke the spell and freed the kingdom was the kiss and embrace between the sisters! I'm tearing up as I write this! It was a selfless act and all that was bad literally melted away. I felt like God was telling me that not only does love conquer all, but love heals all.

Like the movie *Frozen*, I have situations in my life where I feel like a curse needs to be broken. I understand the heartache of these two sisters, one feeling lonely and worthless to help herself and the other feeling helpless to heal her sister. In that dark movie theater I heard the voice of God . . . Love! And love is what we want. Love is the only way to a true happy ending. These Disney storytellers have no idea they are using their gifts and spreading the gospel of Jesus. Wow, I'm so cheesy right now. Note to self: Don't watch Disney cartoons with my kids when I'm PMSing. I'll end up buying three boxes of popcorn and a large bag of Sour Patch Kids and that's just for me!

Take a MOMENT to think about . . .

1. Do you think it's easier to love your kids unconditionally than others? Why?
2. Have you received a selfless act of true love? Have you given one?

Dear God, Thank You for speaking to me in unexpected places like a movie theater. Thank You for giving me the gift of love through your Son. Thank You that I'm a mom and for helping me understand what unconditional love is. Help me to relay that kind of love to others besides my own precious children, like my husband, friends, and those who don't deserve it. Amen.

I'm Keepin' the Purse

I praise you, for I am fearfully and wonderfully made.
Wonderful are your works; my soul knows it very well.
~ Psalm 139:14 (ESV)

My sister-in-law is what I like to call "fancy." She's pretty and well put together. The kind of woman who has two kids and belongs to a Junior League. For my birthday she always gets me fancy presents, things that I would never buy for myself. I question whether I should keep them or sell them on eBay. This past birthday she got me a Coach purse! My first reaction was "How much cash can I get for this?" I'm not a Coach purse kind of gal. I shop at TJMaxx and nothing in my wardrobe or accessory collection ever costs more than $49.99 (and that better be a pant suit). I've always found it incredibly frivolous for women to spend hundreds of dollars on one bag. I've never purchased anything like that in my life. But thousands of women out there carry these purses and that status symbol means something to them. It brings them great joy, or maybe they actually like the way the bag is made. They are made with great quality material. But for their retail price, it should be stitched in gold and contain extra cash in every side pocket. It's ironic because I live in Los Angeles where women have purses galore. The price of their wardrobe alone could feed a small country. I live in the land of excess, and I'm at every garage sale on Saturday mornings buying used items and haggling over the price of a Crock Pot. This is what brings me joy. I suppose if there was a Coach purse at a garage sale and it was under $5 I might buy it.

For our family Thanksgiving gathering, I decided to put my stuff in the new shiny purple purse with the big Coach emblem on it and bring it with me so my sister-in-law could see I liked it. Then I planned to sell it for cash and go buy three purses and two sweaters at Marshalls. But something happened. I put that beautiful bag on my shoulder and all of a sudden I felt a little happier than I was before. Isn't that insane? A purse bringing someone joy? I loved the design and I have to admit I loved all the compliments I was getting about my "Coach bag." And I realized something—I am a fancy purse kind of gal. If someone wants to bless me with a very beautiful item, I should believe I'm worthy of it. That's how God sees me. I'm not a $5 garage sale hand me down. I'm a beautiful new shiny top of the line model He created in HIS image. I don't have to have some false humility that I can't occasionally have extravagant things.

I think most of us moms think it's wrong to do nice things for ourselves, thinking we're someone who should always be humble. Maybe God wants to bless our socks off and let us know it's more than okay to get a manicure and a massage in the same year! We need to stop feeling bad when God wants us to feel cherished, pampered, and special. If a shiny purse or a pair of high heel shoes puts a spring in your step, work those heels girl! God created you to rock it! You still got it and show your kids and family that "Mommy's Still the Hot Chick"! Maybe it will inspire your husband to get out of his sweat pants from 1987 and take you out in public to a restaurant that has menus you can't color on!

Take a MOMENT to think about . . .

1. What is your one splurge item you'd buy for yourself if money was no object?
2. Have you ever gotten a gift so fancy you thought you didn't deserve it? What did you do? Would you do it differently today?

Dear God, Help me to see myself as You see me: shiny, new, and beautiful, even on days when I feel haggard, tired, and completely spent. Help me to realize how much You value me just for who I am no matter what I do. Thank You for allowing me the grace to treat myself to something special and not feel guilty about it. Amen.

Nutella Binges

Train up a child in the way he should go; even when he is old he will not depart from it. ~ *Proverbs 22:6 (ESV)*

Mama said there'd be days like this. I can't take it today. I really can't. I know it's bad because I bought some chocolate Nutella this morning, and I've been sticking my finger in it like a crack addict all day trying to control myself from injuring one of my "beautiful children." Somehow dipping my finger into this rich, creamy chocolate and shoving it in my mouth enables me to not grab a wooden spoon and chase a child around the house. But then again maybe the wooden spoon would help me get more Nutella in my mouth.

I know days like this will pass but right now I've had it. First, at the preschool parent/teacher conference, we were told our three-year-old is stealing food from other kids' lunches and needs to learn "personal space" boundaries. Then, my six-year-old lied to me and said the gummy bears she found on the bottom of the car seat were "fresh." When we came home, I heated up zucchini burgers, potatoes, and some turkey slices and low and behold they both refuse to eat anything. And to top off the day, when I turn my back, my three-year-old became Picasso and DREW ON MY KITCHEN WALL!

I had to discipline her and when she cried it broke my heart into a million pieces. The look of "Mommy, don't you know I did this for you and now you've hurt me and squashed all my dreams of ever becoming a muralist!" After this episode, Lucy throws herself on the floor and says she cannot go back into the kitchen because she saw shadow people on the walls trying to take over her body.

I hid in the bedroom and tried to decompress. I just started my period and I have to get dressed for a Hollywood Gala party where I'm supposed to look hip and none of my pants will button because I'm bloated like Moby Dick. Someone stop me from getting the Nutella and lying in the fetal position and rocking myself to sleep with 80s love songs.

Maybe none of this makes sense to you. If that is the case, put this book down and go celebrate your life because it's not normal. If you've had days like this, just know you are not alone. Hey, I'm not alone. God tells us to raise up our children in the way they should go and they will not depart from it. He just never warned us that it would be this hard. I guess my mother went through days like this. I think that's why she chased me with the fly swatter so much. I guess today is one of the many reasons why God created Nutella. Now, where is that wooden spoon!

Take a MOMENT to think about . . .

1. When you are having a day like this, what is your secret go-to fix?
2. What is the worst thing your kids have done that has sent you over the edge? How did you handle it?

Dear Lord, Help me to control my raging temper on days like this. Help me to find a space to breathe even if it's hiding in the bedroom with my Nutella. I know You see me trying my best. I know tomorrow will be a better day. I love You. Amen.

Top Ten Things Parents Will Never Do Again

1. Take a shower over eleven minutes long . . . alone!

2. Eat at a Five-Star restaurant on a weeknight.

3. Go to Costco or Sam's Club and spend under $300.

4. Leave the house in under twenty-three minutes.

5. Sleep through the night.

6. Watch the news reports about the world and not worry.

7. Wear skinny jeans.

8. Take an unplanned road trip, just for the "fun of it" and not bring snacks.

9. Use the bathroom alone.

10. Wonder why your mother was always tired!

McDonald's Cheeseburgers Are from God

Oh, taste and see that the LORD is good! Blessed is the man who takes refuge in him! ~ Psalm 34:8 (ESV)

Last night I decided I would be brave and take Ruby, Lucy, and Lucy's friend to a Christmas play at a local church. I bravely told my husband he could have the night off.

The craziness started with being stuck in traffic and me being tortured to listen to the entire Chipmunks Christmas album, 345 times. I mean who really cares that all Theodore wants is his two front teeth? (Oh yea, my kids do.) I had my bootleg snacks packed in my purse and my water so I tried to keep them calm. We arrived fifteen minutes late. I wrangled everyone into the back row and Ruby stands on my legs, trying to see the dancing penguins as they sing "Oh Holy Night." After about two minutes, the kids break into my popcorn and start munching loudly. In the middle of the reading of our Savior's birth story, Ruby yells, "Water Mama!" Then Lucy yells, "Mama, I gotta go pceeeeee!" I shuffle them all outside for a potty break and back inside to start this process all over again. As soon as it was over, the kids bolt for the cookies while I tried to say good-bye to several friends. At one point during all this chaos, I literally lost sight of all the kids only to find them ON THE STAGE putting on their own performance of "Santa Baby," causing quite the scene. The big finale was me chasing them off the stage and shoving them into the car like a kidnapper. They were so hyper my head felt like it was going to come off.

I did what any other self-respecting mother would do, I said, "If you guys be quiet, I'll get you all McDonalds!" Let's face it, there is something in those cheeseburgers that make everyone happy. It's a bit of "crack" if you ask me. Five minutes later there was total peace in my car as the kids devoured the French fries and burgers. I even ordered one. As I bit into that processed meat product excuse for a burger, I slipped into my own carb coma. I was in heaven for eight whole minutes until all I can hear in the back is "She stole my toy from my Happy Meal! MOOOOOOOOM!"

I just pretended the noise was not happening and I kept sipping on my Coca Cola, singing "Joy to the World." I do believe God created cheeseburgers for moments like this. I know it would be nice if my kids only ate organic and we churned our own butter. But let's face it, the only people that do that are hipsters with no kids. There is nothing wrong in times of crisis with soliciting the help of a God ordained Happy Meal.

But joking aside, my kids got filled up that night with more than burgers. The play fed them the Word of God and as we rode home, we sang "Joy to the World, the Lord has come." In the end, I realized that things like Happy Meals are enjoyable for a quick fix. I know it can be harder to dig into your Bible than a juicy cheeseburger. But the effects of God's Word are more lasting and calorie free. I think a mix of both of them is never a bad idea.

Take a MOMENT to think about . . .

1. Are you feeding your kids the Word of God?
2. What are some things that seem more appetizing than God's Word in your life?

Dear God, Give me the desire to feed on Your Word more than I desire the quick fixes of this world. Give me an appetite to know You more and a bitter taste for all the things that aren't good for me. Thank You for giving me grace in times of chaos and for creating those heavenly Golden Arches . . . McDonalds! Amen.

Don't Call Me, Tag Me

Jesus looked at them and said, "With man this is impossible, but with God all things are possible." ~ Matthew 19:26 (ESV)

I have a confession to make. I had two completely free days without kids in which I had grand plans to spend the quality time with the Lord. Instead, I got up and greeted the day with my iPhone in hand instead of my Bible. It's literally the first thing I reach for in the mornings to check e-mail, phone messages, text messages, Facebook, Twitter, and Instagram. I know I sound like an addict and I realized it's more of a problem than I'd like to admit. I can judge those that reach for drugs like it's some huge issue and never look at myself. Maybe I should put my phone in my Bible so at least there's a fighting chance my eyes might glance at a verse first thing in the morning. Isn't that pathetic?

I'm actually really embarrassed. I break the law and check my messages when I'm at stoplights. Yeah, go ahead call the cops. I've already been ticketed . . . twice! When will I learn? I know it's illegal, but for some reason I can't live fourteen seconds without checking to see how many people like my new haircut. We're not living moment by moment anymore, we're "tagging them!" I fear the day when my children realize I've been exploiting every milestone, every precious moment in their entire childhood and sharing it with a few thousand of my closest friends for validation that I'm a good mom. Even tonight when my kids were cuddled up in bed with each other, I made a beeline for my phone to "capture" the moment and then blast it to the world. What type of mother does that? Well, a bunch of us apparently. We even take pics of our kids when they're sleeping. When will the madness end?

It's like we can't even make decisions anymore without consulting the "tribal council" of almost strangers that we have accepted as "friends" on social media. It's a game; it's a rush; it's not good. Yes, I also read all the Bible verses people post, but don't think I'm not skimming them to get 12 Holistic Remedies for Dandruff Using Rosemary Oil.

We live in a society where nobody picks up the phone to talk to each other anymore, but we can stare into the wee hours of the night at our ex-boyfriend's pictures. The Internet has become a social watering hole where we post news. There is a fading boundary on what is too personal to talk about. People post deaths, illnesses, prayer requests. We can read marriage arguments that are actually being fought right there online. Before we know it, hours of our lives have been sucked away and what do we have to show for it? Tired eyes! All the stuff I'm reading seems innocent enough, but I'm fearful when my kids have access to all this Internet insanity. How will I protect them? If Mommy is this bad now, how will I set healthy boundaries later? What kind of role model am I being when I'm constantly on my phone?

I want it to stop. I really do. But not badly enough to take any serious action. I can stay off the Internet for a couple days, but then I break into cold sweats and my body starts to go into withdrawal. I feel like the world is passing me by and I'm not online to "experience it." Does any of this ring true to you? Be honest. How much of your life is lived "on the Internet" versus real life. How many moments in your life have you just had to "capture" for all the world to comment. Why should my self-esteem be based on what Ethel in Idaho thinks about my children's Easter dresses? And the driving thing is nothing short of stupid and dangerous. I need to make some changes and I am admitting to you right now I'm scared. Maybe it's not social media but something else that is literally sucking the life out of you. Ask God right now to reveal to you what it might be and if you want to see change, pray with me. For nothing is impossible with God.

Take a MOMENT to think about . . .

1. So what is your thing . . . your time waster? How are you dealing with keeping it in check?
2. If you want to make changes, what is one thing you can do right now to find some balance?

Dear Father God, I'm in over my head and I need Your deliverance. I don't want to look back on my kids' childhood and know that I missed a good chunk of it because my eyes were diverted to a computer screen or iPhone. Show me how to be "present" for my kids and break my addiction to validation from the world. Help me to be as passionate about You as I am the things of this world. I know with You I can do it. I want to start now. Amen.

The Faith of a Child

"Because of your little faith. For truly, I say to you, if you have faith like a grain of mustard seed, you will say to this mountain, 'Move from here to there,' and it will move, and nothing will be impossible for you." ~ Matthew 17:20 (ESV)

I've always done my best to instill great faith in my children from a very young age. My mother and her mother did the same thing. I found several old 1980s Bible cartoons telling Old and New Testament stories on cable. Trying to instill good morals and values, I let the kids watch them and they eat them up. What I didn't realize was that the videos were not as politically correct as videos in the marketplace today. For example, the story of Joseph and Potifer's wife and how she tried to seduce him. The videos actually showed that entire scene. After watching the video, Lucy was playing in her room, playing dress up in her sequined gown and boa, talking to her boy doll. In her deepest five-year-old voice, she said "Joseph . . . why don't you come over and see me sometime!" Who was she, Mae West? Ron, my husband, saw the whole thing and came and got me. We didn't realize she was playing "Potifer's wife!" Out of all the Bible characters, this is the one that draws her attention as a role model? Lord, help us.

We didn't want to make a big deal about it, except to tell all of our friends the funny anecdote. I mean, isn't the whole point of moments like these is so you can have a good story? Well about a week later, I caught her jumping from the top of the bathtub and leaping into the water. She was doing it over and over before I put a stop to it. She immediately started bawling. I said "What's wrong honey? You know that's dangerous!" She sobbed, "Mommy, I was trying to walk on water. Jesus said if I have the faith of a mustard tree anything is possible. I have the faith Mommy. Why did Peter get to walk on water when he didn't even practice?" I smiled and said, "Lucy, if anyone has the faith to walk on water it's you. I believe in you but let's practice on dry land for a while." Lucy has always been a child with bold faith and as much as I'd like to take credit, it's a gift from God. I knew it when her first goldfish died and

I caught her trying to raise him from the dead. "Rise up Goldie! In the name of Jesus, rise up!" Auntie Lori had to have a funeral with Lucy and Goldie in the bathroom in *Finding Nemo* fashion. "All roads lead to the ocean."

How do I, as a mother, foster my child's faith in the impossible while still teaching her to live in a fallen world? Every time she has an "owie" I pray with her. Today she hurt her nose and after I prayed I asked her if the pain was gone. She said, "Mommy when we pray it always goes right away." Man, I want the faith of my child. My wish for her is that she always lives with this pure, unfiltered belief that what the Bible tells me is true. God is our healer yesterday, today, and tomorrow. Lucy doesn't walk by anyone in a wheelchair without offering to pray them out of it. It's been a bit controversial at times, but I wouldn't have it any other way. I appreciate God giving us teachers of how to live as Christ and we call them children.

Take a MOMENT to think about . . .

1. Do you see the pure faith of your children in God's power? In what ways?
2. How can you be more childlike in your faith in God?

Dear Lord, Thank You for the faith of my children. Help me to raise them up in Your Word and continue to teach them that all things are possible for those who love You. Forgive me for my jaded unbelief at times and allow me to see You the way my kids do. Amen.

Top Ten Things Never to Say to a Woman in Labor

1. Do you mind if I watch some TV?

2. When are you thinking about having another baby?

3. When do you plan to start working out again?

4. Oh come on, it can't hurt that bad.

5. I'll be right back, I'm going to get some sushi.

6. I'm here for you. We're in this together. I feel your pain.

7. Just breathe!

8. You're not really going to name the baby that are you?

9. Well, you got yourself into this situation!

10. Smile for the camera!

Precious Jewels

"She is more precious than jewels, and nothing you desire
can compare with her." ~ Proverbs 3:15 (ESV)

I was always very close to my grandmother. Her name
was Catherine Pomarolli, but loved ones called her Kitty.
She was a strong Irish girl, born in 1914. Being the oldest
of ten kids, she was raised in Indiana. She had the mom
gene from birth and a gift for taking care of people, especially with her cooking. When we'd come over for Sunday
dinner, there was always enough food to feed an army. I do
not think she knew how to cook for fewer than fifteen peo
ple. Whether it was her homemade vegetable soup or her
stuffed eggplant, grandma's kitchen was always filled with
the smells of love. I use to watch her peel one hundred potatoes and not even break a sweat. On Christmas Eve she'd

partner up with my other grandmother and spend hours upon hours making a holiday turkey and stuffing feast.

I have a million memories of my grandma. Some I thought were mortifying, like the time she made me sit next to Thomas Johnson so we could hold hands during the "Our Father." Or all the times she interviewed the boys who were calling my house before handing me the phone. My grandparents met on the dance floor at the Greystone Ballroom in Detroit. My grandfather took one look at her, asked her to dance, which continued for sixty years of marriage. They raised two boys and overcame a lot of storms. I've seen pictures of Kitty in her younger days, all dazzled up with her high heels and sparkly jewels. But for me, I mostly remember her standing in the kitchen over the sink or letting me brush her thick beautiful white hair while we watched *Love Boat* and *Fantasy Island* on Saturday nights. She was my buddy and I miss her. A long fight with Alzheimer's disease took her from us about eighteen years ago. A part of my heart is still missing since she left. I know she's in heaven probably cooking for Jesus and about a thousand of His disciples, and I'm sure my Grandpa Eli is up there following her around as well. I do hope there is a ballroom dance floor where my grandparents can strut their stuff.

Precious Jewels

I was recently home visiting my parents and my dad presented me with a box, and inside it was my grandmother's jewelry that she wore in the 1930s. Pearl necklaces with diamonds and feathers, silver chains with pill boxes attached, beads and beads of colored stones, and the most exquisite broaches you've ever seen. I took each and every jewel in my hands, again trying them on just like I remember doing when I was six-years-old. I have a five-year-old little princess named Lucy. She came running over and asked if she could try on one of the special necklaces and I put a pretty yellow one around her neck. Her face lit up because she knew who it originally belonged to. It's funny because the wedding ring on my finger actually belonged to my grandmother. We had it resized and reset; but when someone compliments the beautiful diamond, I tell them it belonged to her first.

I gathered up all my precious new jewels and took them home with me. I felt as if I was given a part of my grandma back to me as I put each new gem into my own jewelry box. The hole in my heart felt a bit smaller. When I put a piece of her jewelry on, it's like I am carrying a piece of history with me, one that I will pass on to my own daughters one day. I will continue to teach them about their great-grandmother and her legacy. I carry these memories with me in my heart; her laugh, her joking, the time we walked all the way to church on a Saturday night for my Sunday school class party and we forgot her homemade cookies so we walked all the way home and back to get them. Sometimes God winks at us and gives us an unexpected gift, like these precious jewels. I know that's what she was to me. And now I have my littlest baby girl, Ruby Joy, which means "God's precious gem," and Lucy which means "Bringer of Light," as the sparkling gems in my life.

Take a MOMENT to think about . . .

1. Do you have any legacies you're sharing with your children from your family history?
2. What are the precious jewels in your life today? How are you treasuring them?

Dear God, Thank You for putting jewels in my life. Help me to honor the legacy set forth before me to be a mother of strength and grace and relying on You for wisdom, just the way my grandmothers did. Amen.

Mirror Mirror in My Car

"Above all, keep loving one another earnestly, since love covers a multitude of sins." ~ 1 Peter 4:8 (ESV)

It was a glorious morning. Lucy and I cuddled as we watched Bible story videos together. Then we got her ready for her very busy day.

As Lucy and I were riding in the car, she said to me, "Mommy, you know how I get cranky sometimes?" "Yes," I said. "Ya wanna know why? It's because I just can't stop thinking about all the bad things you've done to me!" "Say what?" I replied. "Yeah, I just can't get them out of my head."

It's 9:00 a.m. I'm driving her to a play date, and then I'm picking her up and taking her to a hula lesson. Then as a special surprise, I got her tickets to a play that night.

I ask, "So Lucy, what things?" "Well, first you didn't let me get that balloon for my birthday, then you ate the last cupcake, and you didn't let me ride the roller coaster!"

First of all the balloon was a nine-dollar balloon at Disneyland and that is where this horrible mother took her for her birthday. And all she remembers is that she didn't ride the roller coaster and didn't get the balloon! The cupcake thing happened at least two years ago, but I'm glad to know the *one* time I actually got a bite of her sweets it was a travesty that has haunted her for literally years.

I replied the way my mother used to, "Well Lucy, if I'm such a bad mother maybe I should cancel our surprise tonight. Maybe I'll just take your sister." Then it got even worse because I was on a roll. "Do you want to play this game? First of all, you drew on my wall with marker, you bit me and all of your friends at one point or another, and you snuck into my bed and peed in my bed last night . . . need I go on?"

LUCY: I never bit you!

ME: Yes you did! You even bit my friend's cat!

LUCY: Well I just can't get all of this out of my head no matter how hard I try.

ME: Why don't you think about all the good things I've done for you?

LUCY: I can't think of anything.

ME (voice raising, blood boiling): Are you kidding me? You can't remember anything, like the fact that I carried you in my belly, I bathed you, clothed you, and go on the Internet to look for your favorite toys so I can buy them for you? Make your favorite snacks and take you to Disneyland?

LUCY: (No response.)

ME: You better check yourself before you wreck yourself.

ME (holding back tears not believing a six-year-old could get to me so badly): You are so mean, and maybe I've spoiled you too much and that's your problem. (Now I'm out of control and I can't stop the verbal freight train. I'm trying to pull it back so I don't scar her for life.) You want to say things to hurt me? Go ahead but you better check your heart 'cause I'm a person and I matter! And you know what else? I'm gonna take all your presents from Santa and . . . and . . . throw them . . . to . . . the orphans!

LUCY: (Bawling!)

ME: (semi-crying)

I pull the car over. Go hug her.

ME: I'm sorry Lucy. I love you.

LUCY: I forgive you!

After all that, I'm the one apologizing? She's good!

After I dropped her off, I was driving home praying about the conversation. God shot me a lightning bolt revelation: Kerri, that is exactly what you do with your husband. You talk to him in those same tones and keep a record of his wrongs to be brought up at a later date as some excuse for your behavior. Do you see now how ridiculous it sounds?

ME: But God, Ron really did forget to mail our thank you notes after our wedding and it still haunts me!

GOD: Kerri, the apple does not fall far from the tree, My darling. The thing I'm trying to teach you is simple. Love covers a multitude of sins. Forgiveness is not a feeling, it's a choice.

He's got me! I can't believe how sneaky God is. He used my own kid to teach me a marriage lesson. I may change my ways, but I'm sure not telling Ron about this!

Take a MOMENT to think about . . .

1. Has God ever used your kids to reflect your own bad behaviors? How so?
2. Did it make you want to change your ways?

God, Thank You for showing me my own childish behaviors. Thank You for my children being a reflection of me: good, bad, and ugly. Help me not just to forgive, but to forget and concentrate on all the good in my family. Amen.

Bald Is Beautiful

"Therefore I tell you, do not worry about your life, what you will eat or drink; or about your body, what you will wear. Is not life more than food, and the body more than clothes? Look at the birds of the air; they do not sow or reap or store away in barns, and yet your heavenly Father feeds them. Are you not much more valuable than they?"
~ Matthew 6:25–26 (NIV)

I found this letter I wrote to my daughter Lucy when she was five months old:

Dear June Bug,

You and I are balding! We're in this together. We both came into this world with a lot of hair and a cool Mohawk. You still have yours but the rest of your head is suffering. These days you're still my beauty queen, but honey your hair looks like a cross between Albert Einstein and the Nutty Professor! So much of your hair is gone we have to do the old man "comb over!"

I just started losing hair in the shower by the handful. My hormones are running amuck! It's pretty emotional for me and I keep running out with fistfuls of hair yelling at your daddy, "Look! Look! I'm going bald! The sky is falling! The sky is falling!" So I know I sound like a raving lunatic but I think anyone can understand that our hair is a hot commodity and we'd like to keep as much of it as possible. I read that many moms experience the exact same thing. I just thought it wouldn't happen to me. I hate the unknown. I hate not knowing if and when my hair will stop falling out in mass amounts.

But the thing that makes me laugh in all of this hair loss drama is that you, as usual, don't seem to care at all. The more I get to know you and your happy-go-lucky attitude, the more I aspire to be like you. You smile when you're fed and after a nice long nap you wake up ready to face the world. Whether you're in your favorite hand-me-down PJs or some ridiculous sequined number your mother has forced you to wear, you still know you're a star. I pray to God you never ever lose that attitude. I don't want the world and all its fashion magazines to *influence you to think you're anything less than perfect in every way. God made you amazing and I don't want you to come home from school someday and think your body isn't flawless. I think my heart will break if I ever see that you are sad. I don't care that your thighs are chubby. You have these delicious rolls on your belly that everyone wants to take a bite out of. I wonder if that bothers you. I don't think I'd like people biting my stomach.*

What is your secret, Lucy? Can I join you in your world for just one day? Can I put away the worries about my chubby thighs and come lie in your crib and stare at the Winnie the Pooh mobile and drift off to a peaceful dreamland? Maybe I should stop trying to fit into sexy lingerie or skinny jeans and just wear flannel footy pajamas all day long? I'll ask your dad what he thinks. It's not like he's trying to fit into skinny jeans or sexy lingerie. (Sorry for that visual.)

I think if I was five-months-old and no one told me having hair was a big deal, I could relax a lot more. I am so amazed every day as I watch you take on life's big challenges with total peace.

I love you,
Mom

So the end of the story is I lost the chubby thighs and so did Lucy. I got all my hair back and it looked better than ever. I looked so good I got pregnant again with Lucy's sister. And here I sit today with chubby thighs and hair falling out running around my house saying, "Daddy, the sky is falling! The sky is falling and so is all my hair!" When will I learn to relax and be more like my kids? Lucy still takes on challenges with ease. She's so confident most days she thinks she can fly. Maybe she can. I would not doubt it. I suppose God put these children in my life for me to learn from them. They are like the sparrows that Jesus talked about who didn't worry about what they would eat, drink, or wear. They always know they are provided for, and they never lose all their feathers.

Take a MOMENT to think about . . .

1. What is that one thing that you're worried about but you'd like to surrender to God?

2. What would help you surrender to the baggage you carry around each and every day? What steps can you take to help you?

Dear God, Please help me to be more like a sparrow and remember how much more valuable I am to You. Remind me that every hair on my head is numbered. Help me to be more like my kids and after a nice long nap feel rested and ready to take on my day. And God, if You're able, can You make it possible for me to have more nap times? Or any nap times? Amen.

Top Ten Things to Do While Breastfeeding

1. Plan your next vacation, without children.

2. Wonder who movie stars and super models hire as their "wet nurses" and how you could get their numbers.

3. Ask God why, if women carry the babies, men can't do the breastfeeding?

4. Play the minute game with the clock by closing your eyes and seeing how close you can come to sixty seconds without peeking.

5. Remember what it was like to wear tiny lacy bras and wonder who has a number for a good plastic surgeon.

6. Think of all the chores that need to be done around the house and shout them off to your spouse loudly

one by one, starting each sentence with, "Honey, since I'm breastfeeding your child could you . . ."

7. Make important business calls knowing this will be the one time your baby is quiet.

8. Realize your ballet dancing career will probably never happen and you're okay with this fact. You'd freeze in those leggings anyway.

9. Vow never to do a topless scene in any movie even if Matt Damon is your co-star and the money will send your kids to college. (Not that anyone has asked you.)

10. Look lovingly at your baby remembering that you will remind them weekly for the rest of their lives all the sacrifices you've made for them as their mother and they owe you big time!

Quiet Time for Moms

"Be still, and know that I am God."
· Psalm 46:10 (NIV)

One of my goals that I have never truly met is mastering the art of "Quiet Time with God." I meet these women, who seem so put together and happy, as if Jesus and the angels themselves got them out of bed with praise music. When I ask them what their secret is, most of them say, "Quiet time with the Lord." Some of them say, "Xanax!" I don't judge.

I've been trying to master this illusive quiet time. Yes, this might be the only time I'm not physically being pulled in fifty different directions, but these are not my best moments. I'm cranky because I usually wake up with some kind of ache from a ridiculous new workout routine

I have tried. I'm half asleep because I've been awakened three times during the night for no good reason except imbalanced hormones or restless children that need water.

By my bed, I have:

1. The Bible I've owned since the third grade.
2. The Bible translated into a novel.
3. Two books about living a more prosperous life in Christ.
4. One book on the power of a praying mom and the power of a praying parent.
5. Four magazines.
6. A wrap thing I was going to wear to make my stomach skinnier.
7. Mom's One Line a Day Journal, which hasn't been written in for over six months.
8. My CD player with praise music.
9. Twelve pieces of paper with daily mantra prayers I'm supposed to say for my family.
10. My cell phone that includes four Bible apps, but more importantly my e-mails and Facebook.

Do you want to guess which one I'm reaching for first?

Yes, number ten! If you think I'm horrible, put this book down and go read something by another famous author. Now for the rest of you heathens, let's work on this together.

It's not for lack of trying that my "quiet times" seem to fail. I just can't shut off all the loud noises in my head. I try to pick up the Bible and start reading. I'll get into a chapter about King David and that will remind me of Lucy's play date with David Gurman and the fact that we need to buy a birthday present for his brother. Then the mental roller coaster has taken off, and I try to get back to my daily meditations with God. I pull out a prayer. I start pleading the blood of Jesus over my family and that reminds me there was laundry left in the washer overnight and I wonder if I'll have to do the whole load over again. At this point at least one child needs my attention and only half of my family has been prayed over before I need to get out of bed. I pray to God to help me make it through one more day. I thank Him that I'm alive and that I'm healthy. I try my best to pray for the people on my prayer list, especially those I promised I'd be interceding for and all those others who catch my heart. I think of my friend Janine in Africa, who is literally rescuing babies out of trash cans, and I look at the pictures of her beautiful babies on my phone and for a moment I am calm and God leads me to pray for that child who is surviving against insurmountable odds. I pray for Janine and her staff and thank God for her selfless devotion to saving these kids. I thank God that my kids are not lying in a garbage dump.

As I walk into the girls' room, I'm greeted by the biggest smile you've ever seen from my baby, Ruby Joy. My prayer doesn't really end, it just gets louder with giggles and squeals and morning songs and dances. Maybe it's not so bad after all, and maybe God sees my heart more than the preciseness of my morning routine. I talk to Him throughout my day and never miss a chance to pray if someone needs it. So come to think of it, maybe my quiet time is a little louder than others, but I love the Lord with all my heart. I couldn't make it through this motherhood jungle without Him. And one day when my kids are gone and there are no squeals to wake me, I will sit quietly with my Bible and I will scream loudly, "GOOOOOD, I miss my kids and the chaos!"

Take a MOMENT to think about . . .

1. What does your daily routine look like?
   How much of it includes time with God?
2. Are there any changes you want to make?
   Ask Him to help you.

Lord, Thank You for looking at my heart and knowing it is pure. Thank You for creating me to praise You through chaos, and I always know I can turn to You for guidance. Amen.

Lies My Daughter Told Me

"The Lord detests lying lips, but he delights in people who are trustworthy." ~ Proverbs 12:22 (NIV)

The other day Lucy said to me, "Mommy, do you want to hear the song I sing when I'm scared?" She launched into this adorable creative tune about fluffy cats and candy canes and other things that ease your pain.

I said, "Lucy, that is wonderful. Where did you learn that?"

"I made it up!" she said.

I immediately start planning her audition for *America's Got Talent* as singer/songwriter extraordinaire, only regretting I haven't started her in piano yet at age six. We may be too late.

So this morning while Lucy's out, Ruby and I turn on some morning cartoons. I see an animated boy singing

"Fluffy Cats and Candy Canes and Other Things to Ease My Pain." First I try to figure out how this boy stole Lucy's song, and then I came to my senses. That little kid lied to me! I can't believe it. But wait, who am I kidding? This was the child at two-years-old who poured a glass of water into her kiddie potty and said, "Look Ma Ma, I go pee pee! I want treat!"

Then at three, when her father told her not to wet her pants, while jumping on the trampoline she had an accident. (How can I blame her? I've had two kids and I can't jump on the trampoline without having an accident either.) Her father was so mad. He said, "Lucy, what happened?"

Lucy: "Well Daddy, there was this big rain cloud and it came and hit me in the butt!" Ron was laughing so hard he could only utter, "Well, that is the last time you are allowed to play with rain clouds."

Sometimes it's hard to keep a straight face as a parent. As mad as I am at her for lying, I keep getting flashbacks of my own childhood, like the time my mother went to my kindergarten teacher conference to find out that I'd told everyone she drove a Lincoln town car and was my chauffeur.

In third grade I told everyone I was dating John Schneider because I had an autographed picture my grandma got me and it said, "To Kerri, I love ya!" That was child's play compared to the time I convinced my entire junior high that my dad set me up with Corey Feldman (from the greatest movie of all time, *The Goonies*), and he was coming to my birthday party! It was too easy. These were kids in my Dutch Christian reformed school in Michigan. I was the only entertainment they had! (On a side note, I did meet Corey Feldman fifteen years later when he came to my book launch party.)

What am I going to do about this lying epidemic? I don't want her to end up in prison after a life of hard crime! I've prayed with my daughter, punished her, and told her lying was the worst thing she can ever do. But it seems to come so easy for her. Did I genetically predisposition her to be the "lying kid"? Is this normal?

I don't have the answers and I know lying is a sin. I suppose motherhood is filled with one challenge after another. I don't know why I keep hoping we're over them all and she's only six.

When I did ask her about it, she did say to me, "Mommy, I'm sorry for the misunderstanding but the line about Dandelions and Ice Cream was mine. So technically I wrote some of the song!" She's good. She's really good. She'll make a great lawyer some day!

Take a MOMENT to think about . . .

1. Has your child gone through a lying phase? How long did it last and how did you handle it?

2. Is your child going through something right now you just don't know how to stop? Ask God to help you with creative strategy.

Dear God, I don't know how to handle my child today. Can You please help me find the right words that speak to their heart? Can You help me discipline them in love but also lay a firm foundation of Your truths? I have no idea how to start so I need Your help. I know You will provide the answers. You always do. Amen.

Mommy Magic

"As a mother comforts her child, so will
I comfort you." ~ Isaiah 66:13 (NIV)

One of the perks of become a mom is that you get magical powers. No one tells you about this beforehand. I think it's some sort of reward for surviving the pregnancy and birth. A good example of this is outlined in a letter that I wrote to my daughter Lucy when she was first born:

Little Bug,

You were so sad and crying uncontrollably today. People said you were "teething" or a myriad of other issues, but all I know is that when I stuck my pinky finger in your mouth you happily accepted it and then sucked and sucked with all your might. You smiled at me as if to say, "Thanks Mom!" and then you closed your eyes in pure bliss and drifted off to dreamland. I realize I have power in my little finger. I can make it all better. If only I could keep that "magic finger" for when your first boyfriend breaks up with you, when the other girls don't pick you for their kickball team, or any of the other terrors I fear you will have to face. Oh, it can be so hard. I know this from firsthand experience.

You'll probably be blessed with my sense of humor, which has been described as "inappropriate or lethal wit" at times. That will get you into trouble. The rule of thumb my dear is "sometimes we think things that are funny in our heads, but we don't have to say them out loud!" As I watch you sleeping and kiss your forehead, I wish there was a way for me to permanently attach my lips to your soft little brow for the next twenty years. I wonder if my mom felt that way about me. I wonder if she thought her kisses could bring healing throughout my childhood and growing up years. I know there is nothing quite like a mother's hug or even now a mother's encouraging words. I think that is why so many daughters just crave to hear the words "I'm so proud you're my daughter" from their own moms, even when we're all grown up.

You, my dear, will always be my little baby. I will always want to be there to make the bad things in this

*world go away. I'll use my pinky finger, my lips, my mind,
or my whole body if needed to shield you from harm and
heartache. I wish my kisses could be shields that will keep
you from ever being hurt. I just want you to know as
long as I'm able and on this earth, I'll keep kissing you
and singing you made up lullabies (because I don't know
the words to the real ones). I'll keep pulling the car over
to make sure you're still breathing when you're quiet. I'll
keep rocking you at 3:00 a.m. and doing whatever I can
to make your tears go away. Even when you're thirty-three.*

> *Love,*
>
> *Mom*

I loved finding this letter because as cheesy as this
sounds, it's still true. I still have my "mommy powers"
when my kids are hurting. No one can put a Band-Aid on
better than I can because I seal it with a prayer. No one
can kiss an owie away better than I can. No one can cheer
louder than I can at a school play or soccer game to make
my child's face light up like a Christmas tree. We hold the
key to our kids' hearts in so many ways and not just when
they're babies.

Even today when I, as an adult, get good news, I want
to hear the words "good job" from my mom. If I do something that disappoints my mom, I want to fix it right away.

I want my kids to feel that way about God too. I want them to know God is cheering for them even more than I am. And I want them to know God's infinite love. I don't think I truly understood unconditional love until I became a mother, and even then it's not even in the same stratosphere as God's unconditional love. I understand that nothing I do is ever going to take God's love away from me. He loves me because He loves me because He loves me.

Take a MOMENT to think about . . .

1. Can you think of a moment with your kids when you felt like you had "mommy powers" and no one else could comfort them but you?
2. How did that make you feel?

Dear Lord, Thank You for Your unconditional love. Help me to love the way that You love, even when the kids write on the walls with purple sharpie, or flush a roll of toilet paper down the toilet. Give me the patience and understanding that You so freely give to me. Help me to be a better wife and mother to my family. Amen.

Top Ten Signs You Need a Moms' Night Out

1. You think bath night applies to you as well as the kids, and actually contemplate climbing in the tub just to save time.

2. Your hairdresser thinks you died because she hasn't seen you since you got pregnant.

3. You're beginning to look European when it comes to the whole "no shaving" thing.

4. The last movie you saw in the theater was *You've Got Mail* with Meg Ryan.

5. The only magazine you've read in the last five years is *Highlights* and you think it's a tabloid.

6. When you call to order a pizza, they know your name and ask how your kids are doing.

7. Your kids left the room and you kept watching *Dora the Explorer* to find out if she got to her destination all right.

8. Your sweatpants have replaced all the other pants in your wardrobe and you're fine with it.

9. You're wearing nursing bras and you stopped nursing twelve months ago.

10. Because you're an awesome mom and you deserve it!

Chick Flicks and Happy Endings

I know what it is to be in need, and I know what it is to have plenty. I have learned the secret of being content in any and every situation, whether well fed or hungry, whether living in plenty or in want. I can do all this through him who gives me strength. ~ Philippians 4:12–13 (NIV)

When I was single I wrote a piece titled *Why I Don't Watch Chick Flicks* explaining why they are bad for women. I expressed how the films are hurting our society by portraying relationships in an unrealistic way. These films have also caused me to go into a serious chocolate chip cookie binge. Real life never works itself out in ninety minutes, and I myself have never been picked up by a guy in a horse-drawn carriage.

However, I did fall in love with a guy who offered me chocolate chip cookies! I did get married and walk down the aisle in a rented pretty white dress. It didn't take ninety minutes; it took thirty-two years.

But tonight, after another long exhausting day of chasing my kids and folding 343 loads of laundry, I found myself engrossed in *You've Got Mail*, which stars all time favorite chick flick actors, Tom Hanks and Meg Ryan. Yeah, I'm old school. Meg was the ultimate romantic. At the end of the movie Tom and Meg find out that they really are meant to be together, and when they embrace, I'm a goner. I can't help but notice I've got the same goose bumps I had the first time I saw this cheesy film and the same tear rolling down my left cheek. I'm just so happy for Meg because she was lonely and then she found her true love. God bless her! She gets me every time.

My point is that these movies can't be taken from the shelves because like it or not we need them. Yes, I said it! We live in a bitter sarcastic world full of sickness, financial crisis, and war. But some of us still want to believe in happy endings. Is that so wrong to admit? I grew up with fantasies of what would truly make my dreams come true. I marvel tonight at what true contentment really is. I think I can honestly say I'm content.

I've just recently gone through a very tough time where the love of my life, my husband, was battling an illness. I didn't have my cuddling time, my movie buddy, and my best friend in my home for a while, and it's brought new perspective to the term *happy ending* and "for better or for worse."

My life may look different from a romantic comedy movie and instead of an orchestrated music sound track, my life has *Hickory Dickory Dock* and *Itsy Bitsy Spider*. And instead of passionate sex scenes, my scenes may involve me, my husband, an entire season of *Downton Abbey* on DVD, chocolate ice cream, and cuddling for hours on our big fluffy red couch. I married a guy who likes *Downton Abbey* . . . happy ending right there! It's my own realization that I don't want Tom Hanks or Tom Cruise. I'm truly content with the man God gave me. I'm truly happy with our little world. It's far from perfect and some of our arguments sound more like a "Lifetime Movie of the Week," but it works for us.

So instead of watching Meg with bitterness in my heart, I can enjoy her journey and realize I wouldn't trade places with her or any of her characters. I relish in rooting for the underdog and sometimes I do love a great escape into someone else's life for a couple hours. It's cheesy but I like it! It's a hobby, and for me it's better than scrapbooking or hiking—God forbid! I choose activities that don't interfere with my couch eating.

A huge part of my contentment in life is because I get to be a mom. Thousands of women would give their right arm to have a baby to kiss goodnight. I don't want to take this blessing for granted. I'm a mother and no one can take that away from me. That is part of my happy ending and the rest is unfolding day by day.

No matter what trials you're facing, I challenge you to find some happy endings in your life right now. Life is short. Ask God to give you perspective instead of believing the lies that your life isn't good enough. If God has bestowed upon you the biggest honor of all time and allowed you to be in charge of a human life, that is enough to make you get on your knees and thank Him. If you're alive, and you know you're going to heaven that is enough to feel real joy, not the kind they make up in movies that fade with the credits. I know life isn't easy, but we have the option to find our own "happy ending" right where we are.

Take a MOMENT to think about . . .

1. Do you still watch chick flicks? What is your favorite and why?

2. Can you think of your life as a "happy ending" right where you are? If not, why?

Dear God, Thank You for creating ice cream and romance. Please help me to realize my own happy ending moments in the midst of my crazy days. Help me not to take these days for granted because I know they will go by all too fast. Amen.

Second Child Syndrome

See what great love the Father has lavished on us, that we should be called children of God! And that is what we are! The reason the world does not know us is that it did not know him. ~ 1 John 3:1 (NIV)

If you are a mom with only one child, I know this about you. You are reading this devotional because you really care. You want to be closer to God and a better role model, and you've read books even when you were pregnant to prepare for the gift of motherhood. Let me tell you what is going to happen. Your one perfect child will remain that way until about sixteen months old when he or she will take your mascara and finger paint all over your shower curtain. Then he or she will get kicked out of children's church for biting, and you will consult all of your books to find the only solution . . . Start Over.

Like me you will then have more children and vow to do better, be more diligent, and attentive.

Here is the secret no one is telling you: With each child you care a little less about perfection. Your brain cells have literally been sucked out of you and you've brushed your teeth with Boudreaux Butt Paste at 5:00 a.m. in the morning—twice! Your next child is a prime candidate for what I like to call the Second Child Syndrome. This is where the second child does not get the perks the first one did . . . like food.

They will not have a scrapbook. You will take one photo of the baby and Photoshop in the background elaborate birthday parties and the Eiffel Tower and hope they believe all of this happened before they were two.

The second child is not a nuisance. They are just trying to survive. They will grow up strong because from the moment of their birth they have had to fight their older sibling for everything from toothpaste to the last piece of cake (which they will never get until the older sibling develops a cake allergy or leaves for college). The second child will grow up wise. They will know how to work the system. They will see all the mistakes made by their older sibling and be craftier than you ever thought them capable.

A second child would never cut their own hair because they have seen the wrath of Mommy the day before school pictures. A second child will be more thoughtful for they know that giving Mommy a well-timed hug after she's disciplined the elder child is always a good idea. A second child will grow up bilingual because they will be watching *Dora the Explorer* from the time they come out of the womb. A second child will be full of worldly wisdom because the amount of TV they watch well makes up for the fact you didn't let your first child touch TV until they were three. In fact, the second child is busy watching Lifetime and Food Network right along with you because they are hiding under the couch in complete silence and you forgot they were there. The second child will be potty trained early because they don't like the sensation of their wet diaper dragging the floor. The second child will not grow up with a sense of entitlement because every stitch of clothing they own is a hand me down with missing buttons and sweaters with other siblings names on it.

But the second child will be full of joy and know what it's like to be cherished because the second time around Mommy realizes that it's all going much too fast. You won't be rushing them to walk, because the longer they are in one place the easier it is to find them. You won't be rushing them into toddlerhood because you've seen the future and it is messy. A second child will know what being adored feels like because they have Mom, Dad, and siblings to cuddle them and cheer for them at life's big moments.

They will grow up with a sense of wonder because the people in their home have experienced everything first and are more than willing to share the "tricks." A second child will be a treasure to their mother's heart and always be her baby. Now don't even get me started on those of you that are crazy enough to have a third child. I bet you don't even know where that one is right now!

Take a MOMENT to think about . . .

1. Did you learn anything from raising your first child that helped you with the second or third?

2. What advice do you wish someone had told you before you had kids?

God, Please help me to teach my children well, each as individuals and unique creative beings. Give me energy to cherish each one of them and let them know how much they are loved. Let my babies still want to cuddle with me even when they're twenty-nine! Amen.

I'm Not Fat, It's My Thyroid

Praise the LORD, my soul, and forget not all his benefits—
who forgives all your sins and heals all your diseases.
~ Psalm 103:2–3 (NIV)

I got great news today. My thyroid tests came back low. I knew I wasn't just fat, and now I have something to blame it on. Symptoms of low thyroid include weight gain, irritability, fatigue, and mood swings. This is better than PMS. I have an actual blood test to waive in my husband's face when he catches me throwing a chair through a window someday. (Hey, it's a disease; you never know what I might do.) I've been battling the "bulge" ever since my second kid was born and I don't think three years later still counts as "baby weight." The problem I have is that I live in Los Angeles where I get asked if I'm pregnant about every six weeks because I'm not wearing size 0 Lu Lu Lemon yoga pants.

I have a new respect for women who've struggled to lose weight. I had no idea how difficult it would be. I never listened to the warnings as I was eating my banana splits for dinner that it would be harder after thirty or even after having kids to lose weight. I've tried everything, Zumba, Yoga for seniors (we just lay there the whole hour, and then go to the buffet). I even got a treadmill, which became a clothes rack so we got rid of it. Now I'm searching to buy another one, a better one, one that runs for me! I remember my grandma had that contraption in her bedroom that was like an exercise belt, and it shook your whole body for you while you just stood there. I need one of those!

I'm new at the whole dieting thing and nothing has worked at all. Maybe because I put cocoa powder and Hershey's syrup in the kale shakes? Maybe it's because I secretly eat my kids Halloween candy at 11:00 p.m. when I'm stressed. I've tried supplements, the cellophane wrap thing, and even the darn tummy tuck girdle that is supposed to burn calories. All the girdle did was give me a hernia! I have no will power. I love food. Don't even get me started about the holiday season. There is no way on

God's green Earth someone could possibly lose weight from the months of November to January. It's the season of excess and I don't have an "off button." Party food is wonderful especially because it's unlimited quantities and it's FREE. Tonight, when no one was looking, I ate the entire Brie cheese dip and four logs of peppermint bark. I have plenty of flowy holiday outfits that hide a multitude of sins.

It's important for you to know that I believe in healing. I am a prayer warrior that claims God's promises of healing to every one of us. Psalm 103 is my life verse. He has healed all our diseases. If you had cancer, I'd pray for God to get rid of it, just like I did with my mother. If you were missing a leg, I'd pray for a new one or die trying. But for some reason this thyroid thing was like a relief to me. I knew something was not right with my body, but I have been too busy to go and get a check-up. Aren't we women the worst with that? I had every single symptom of a low thyroid, and when my tests showed there was an issue, instead of praying healing, I just bragged about it to my friends and commiserated about all of their symptoms.

Why would I believe and fight so hard for healing for others but when it comes to myself, I take my diagnosis and wear it like a badge of honor. I prayed about it and I felt like God was saying, "Whose knowledge are you seeking? How much more time have you spent on WebMD than spending time in My Word and listening to My promises of healing for *all* your diseases?"

What was I afraid of? Who am I going to believe? And what am I going to do about it? How far am I willing to put my faith out there? This was just one moment in my life where my faith was tested. I believe God's healing for me is not only for today but for every area of my life. It was time to talk the talk and walk the walk. I'll make that speed walking so I can burn some calories too!

Take a MOMENT to think about . . .

1. How much do you struggle to believe healing is for today and not just in Bible stories?

2. Have you submitted yourself to God's plans, whatever that plan may be? How did that make you feel? Was it hard to release your anxiety and fear?

Dear God, I'm sorry that there are times in my life that I doubt You. I believe that Your promises are for me, as well as for others. Please forgive me for my lack of faith, and please strengthen my walk with You so I will never fear or be anxious in anything. Amen.

This Is 40!

The LORD says: "My thoughts and my ways are not like yours. Just as the heavens are higher than the earth, my thoughts and my ways are higher than yours."
~ Isaiah 55:8–9 (CEV)

Well, it happened; I turned forty. My husband threw me a huge Willie Wonka party with all the fixings. We had chocolate, mounds of other sugar sweets, and grown up treats like prosciutto and melon. It was fun and a bunch of us danced to 80s hip-hop till after midnight. Yes, we're nuts. A lot of these folks were at my 80s dress-up party when I turned thirty. I was single then and had hoped to meet Prince Charming, but the closest I came to meeting Mr. Right was slow dancing with a cute guy dressed in white tennis attire. He told me I was adorable but thought prison would be more fun than church so that ended fairly quickly.

The morning after I turned thirty, I sat in my living room apartment dressed in my favorite flannel pajamas and opened my presents alone. I got a lot of scented candles that year. Turning thirty was a milestone in my life and, even though I had a great party, I was terribly depressed. I had begged God for decades to provide me with someone special to share my "milestones" with. I had been a bridesmaid on too many occasions, and I was so depressed that I had not found my soul mate. All of the "church ladies" would bring their prayer shawls and holy water and try to cast out the demons that were keeping me from "getting a husband"! I told them the demons were called "good taste and high standards"!

Where had I lost my way? Why was God punishing me? Here I was, just turning thirty and I couldn't understand why God had not answered my prayers. I felt so utterly uncertain of my future. I looked up to God, made myself a cup of tea, and skipped church that day. I couldn't face the happy "families" in every pew. I went to the ocean and talked to God instead. I told Him I trusted Him with my life, but I also reminded Him I knew I was ready. I prayed for my future husband. And you know what, not a mere four months later, God answered my prayers with the love of my life.

So, as I celebrated my fortieth birthday, sitting in my living room and opening presents with the help of two crazy daughters, I was reminded how different my life has become. My kids took over the dance floor of my party and we all danced till the wee hours of the night. What a difference a decade makes. The next morning, after the party, we all went to the same beach that I went to when I was thirty. I saw my daughter Lucy writing me love notes in the sand. The sun was shining and for a moment my life felt utterly complete. I could feel the wind blowing softly on my face as if it was God saying to me, "My daughter, My daughter, My love for you is like this ocean. I've seen all your salty tears, and I've washed them away and brought in joy. I heard every heart cry and I never forgot you. My ways are not your ways and My timing is perfect. Thank you for trusting Me, My child. I know it wasn't easy but wasn't it worth it?"

All I could think of, as tears welled up in my eyes was . . YES!

Take a MOMENT to think about . . .

1. Can you remember a time when you felt totally alone? Did you talk to God about it?

2. Is there anything in your life you're begging and pleading with God about? What do you think He's trying to say to you?

3. Have you ever wanted something so badly and then did not obtain it, only to look back later and see that it was good that you did not receive it? Did that strengthen your faith in God?

Dear God, Thank You for putting up with all my whining, begging, and pleading, trying to force my will onto You. Thank You for holding me close when I felt utterly alone. Thank You for all the years I've had on this earth and allowing me to get a tiny bit wiser with each passing one. I doubted You so many times and You still loved me. You never withheld any blessings from me. I'm so grateful. Amen.

Sunday at Home

"For I know the plans I have for you," declares the LORD,
*"plans to prosper you and not to harm you, plans to give you
hope and a future." ~ Jeremiah 29:11*(NIV)

Today was going to be different for this triple Type A
control freak. I had it all planned out. I know of other
moms that cook for their families and prepare lovely meals,
and I was bound and determined to join their ranks, at
least for today. I just wanted to create the perfect Sabbath
and a lovely home cooked meal for my deserving family.

I put the kids down for a nap with the full intent to
start dinner but then remembered that the Olympics
were on TV so I sat down to watch it. The baby woke up
from her nap screaming, so I got her and actually changed
her diaper on time. Sometimes the poor kid's diaper is

sweeping the floor before it's changed. We finished watching the gymnastics competition together, as I pictured her accepting her medal for most flips on a living room couch! I finally endeavored into the kitchen to try to make the recipe. It was this pouch thing that I bought at a craft fair. The lady said that anyone could do it. She obviously had not tried my cooking.

I pulled the raw pieces of chicken out of the fridge, along with the heavy cream, onions, tomatoes, and everything else that was needed. I cut the chicken into little pieces and did everything the recipe said to do. I felt so Martha Stewart, even though I spent twenty-six minutes working on a five-minute recipe. I took a quick break, walking in the living room to watch my perfect baby play, and all of a sudden the kitchen is filled with smoke. Apparently there is a thing called a fan in the oven area I was supposed to use. I was also supposed to stir the chicken. I would like to mention that neither of these things was on the recipe!

As I played firefighter in my kitchen, Lucy walks in with the blow up pool that I had previously purchased. She reminds me, "Mommy, you said you'd let me go swimming today if I didn't hit any kids at church!" I said, "Ask your Daddy to blow it up!" She says, "Why don't you ask him, he's your husband!" Just then Ron walks in the kitchen and a bowl that contained the heavy cream and cornstarch falls to the ground, splattering its contents all over the green kitchen mat. Ron starts laughing and runs out of the room. Lucy starts screaming, "I didn't do it! I didn't do it!" She runs off with her plastic, deflated pool. I'm stuck cleaning up the mess, but first stopping to take pictures for Facebook.

Finally everything is simmering and Lucy asks me to blow up her beach ball because Daddy is too tired after blowing up the pool. I take the ball outside and put Ruby next to Lucy on the slide. I turn my back for ONE second and guess who is in the pool? Ruby, of course. Does it matter that she is fully clothed and in a diaper? My only option is to get in and drag out my wet child. So here I am, wet, covered in some cornstarch mess and smelling of smoke. I had to laugh! We eventually ate dinner and everyone survived.

Yes, sometimes you get more than you bargained for, but aren't those the times that you cherish! You do your best to make plans, but always leave room for a curve ball or four. No matter what it looks like, God knows your heart and He's proud of you for trying. Maybe we as moms won't get the accolades of the world for doing all that is asked of us on a daily basis. And maybe you look at other so-called "perfect" moms and feel like you'll never get it all together. You're not alone and sometimes ya gotta just jump in the baby pool and swim! You are a mother, you are blessed! Words of wisdom though, be careful if you watch the Food Network. The women on those shows can't be human!

Take a MOMENT to think about . . .

1. Can you remember a time when you tried to have a perfect day for your family and it didn't go as planned? How did you handle it? How would you do it different next time?

2. How can you keep from putting undue stress on yourself and your family? Take a few minutes each day to ask God to give you patience and understanding when life seems to unravel.

Dear God, Help me to have a sense of humor when things don't go as planned. Help me to stop and enjoy the moments of this crazy life You've blessed me with. Thank You for seeing all of my efforts when nobody else does. Please give me patience when I'm stressed or tired. Thank You for loving me for who I am and for blessing me with this wonderful family. Amen.

Your Momma Can't Dance and Your Daddy Done Lost Your Shoes

*"Children are a heritage from the LORD,
offspring a reward from him."*
~ Psalm 127:3 (NIV)

Okay, mother of the year here. I went to get my six-year-old daughter's dance clothes so I could pick her up after school and shuffle her off to Ballet/Tap class, so she can further my . . . um, I mean her dreams, of being a professional dancer by the age of nine (or Cirque du Soleil trapeze artist, we're not picky).

It was a typical day and by typical I mean truly insane. A friend needed last minute childcare, so I added an eight-year-old boy to the toddler in our home. He took the liberty of teaching her war games on his iPad, and now she's running around my house looking for weapons. I wish she had this passion for dust and clutter. If only there was some way to channel her super war powers to my advantage. As I searched for Lucy's tutu, tap, and ballet shoes, as you might have guessed, one tutu but no shoes! Ron took her to class last week and when I approached him about where her shoes were, he gave me that ever familiar shrug and said, "I don't know, I think they're in a bag." UGH!

So, I head out, now fifteen minutes late, with a pair of black patent leather shoes, a leotard, and lots of snacks for bribery. I needed a plan. Would I take her to class and explain to the teacher and all the other perfect "dance" moms why Lucy was showing up late without the proper dance footwear? You know, you can be shot for lesser crimes in the dance world. Or, could I make up some elaborate story that Lucy was just too busy training for the kindergarten chess competition so she forgot about her dance class.

While I was in the car scheming, I realized I had a choice. I could let Lucy make the decision. I could present her with the fact that her dance shoes were temporarily lost, and I could let her decide if she wanted to attend the class shoeless or go home and skip it for a week. Secretly I was hoping she'd pick the latter option. I hate having to sit there and pretend to care about all the other moms and nannies lives in the waiting room. And although there is the financial liability to think about (it did cost me $11!), what's the big deal if she skips one class? Yet, I wonder what lesson I am teaching? Is it wrong to sign up for something and not follow through, even if it is inconvenient? Was I making too big a deal about one week of missing class? After all, it wasn't Lucy's fault. I felt guilty of not being the "put together" mom, once again. *Is this ever going to change,* I asked myself silently in the car?

I picked Lucy up and plainly said, "I'm so sorry to disappoint you, Lucy. I have some bad news. I can't find your dance shoes. I did everything in my power to find them, but I just couldn't. I'm so sorry I failed you. Do you still want to go to class?"

Lucy said, "You mean I get to go home instead? I think I need a nap. School was really tiring today. Thanks, Mom. You're the best."

We happily got in the car and I realized that in her eyes I can do no wrong, and she saved me from one whole hour of listening to the Real Life Housewives of Dance! When we arrived home, Ruby and Joe had made a fort in my living room so they could together save the world. Ruby invited us in, showing off her new hand grenades, which curiously looked exactly like tap shoes!

I think I learned something about kids that day. They are much more flexible than we give them credit for. I shouldn't have worried so much about Lucy's reaction before I even experienced it. Why do we do this? Kids are made in the image of God and they have His heart. They're just happy to spend time with us, saving the world with one tap shoe grenade at a time!

Take a MOMENT to think about . . .

1. Can you recall a time your child surprised you with the way they reacted to something? How did it make you feel?

2. As a parent, it's hard for us to let go and not focus on the little things that can upset the apple cart. How can you relinquish the anxiety of not being the "put together mom" that we all so often feel? How can God help you with these feelings?

Dear God, Help me to expect the best in my children instead of worrying about the worst-case scenario. Help me to trust that I'm doing a good job raising them and that they are balanced, well-adjusted little people. Amen.

Top Ten Worst Texts You Can Send Your Wife on Moms' Night Out

1. Do you know where our daughter is?

2. I'm taking the kids to Disney World because they asked.

3. Do we have a fire extinguisher?

4. Dinner was great! Do you have the number for poison control?

5. I didn't know our four-year-old was such a good poker player. My friends love her.

6. Is it okay if the kids and I watch *Breaking Bad*? He is a chemistry teacher, after all.

7. How are you enjoying your movie? We missed you! Turn around! Want some popcorn?

8. Call your mother. She saw your outfit on Facebook and she says it's inappropriate.

9. I think the Lord is leading me to take some time off work to be a stay at home dad. P.S.: I got fired today.

10. This kid stuff is easy! Why are you always complaining? P.S.: Is the baby with you?

Boot Camp and Foxholes

"The LORD is compassionate and gracious, slow to anger, abounding in love. He will not always accuse, nor will he harbor his anger forever; he does not treat us as our sins deserve or repay us according to our iniquities."
~ Psalm 103:8–10 (NIV)

The clock radio in my car strikes 5:40 a.m. as I drive to the YMCA to torture myself in a two-week boot camp because I'm twenty pounds overweight after giving birth to a child who just turned three! Fleetwood Mac's song "Dreams" is playing on the radio. You know the tune: "Thunder only happens when it's rainin' . . . Players only love you when they're playin'." I'm instantly transported to another lifetime as a young, carefree, twenty-three-year-old who was head over heels in love with some Marine she had met while wearing some cute little sundress. If I had only realized then that the lyrics of that great song would be so foreshadowing!

Hearing the song brought every sensory image flooding back to my brain. I was right there again with the wind in my hair. I wasn't driving to boot camp at the YMCA. I was driving to Boot Camp at Camp Pendleton in San Diego. I did a lot of "outreach ministry" at Camp Pendleton. Don't be jealous! I remember walking along cobblestone streets with my Marine, picking flowers from peoples' yards at 1:00 a.m., thinking it was the most romantic moment ever!

My Marine was a charmer, to put it mildly. Yes, he actually did sing, "You Lost That Lovin' Feelin'" on one knee to me one night. But this moment was not about him, it was about the girl I once was. Did I envy her? She seemed so free. I wondered what life would have been like if I ended up with my Marine? We had a dramatic parting, and I think back to when I secretly waited for him to show up somewhere when he "shipped back in" and carry me off like the film *An Officer and a Gentleman*.

I then realized that the girl I was back then is still the girl today, just twenty pounds heavier! I still have some cool little sundresses in my closet. I realized that even my "carefree days" were not so consequence free. I did a lot of stupid stuff that caused me a lot of pain. I sometimes use to beat myself up for my bad past decisions. I thought maybe God was punishing me by making me wait so long to finally get married, but God would never do that. He never let me fall too far away from His loving embrace. He was always there to catch me when I fell. God let me know that no matter what I was going through, I always belonged right there with Him. Now that I'm a wife and mother I consider myself more of a veteran than a new recruit in navigating relationships. I've faced many bigger battles than deciding what dress to wear. I love that Friday nights are now spent with Mexican food on the couch, waiting for the girls to fall asleep so Ron and I can try to make it through an episode of *The Biggest Loser*. I'm with the crew God picked out for me, and it is good.

So, for today, I'll jam out to my Fleetwood Mac and know that I still "got it" (whatever "it" is)! I just know there are three people in this world named Ron, Ruby, and Lucy that think I'm cool! I know how much my Father God and my family love me just the way I am, so I turned the car around with my crankin' tunes and head back to my foxhole (i.e., my bed). I've had enough of boot camp for one lifetime! Wait! We need supplies . . . Hello Krispy Kreme!

What about you? Are you happy with the foxhole you're in today or are you reminiscing about days gone by? I know it's easy to only remember the good things from our past, and they might make our present situations seem a bit unexciting. Just know that God has you with this particular platoon for a specific reason. They are your fighting buddies and it's your job to love, protect, and lay down your life for them. It's a thankless job, but somebody's gotta do it, and remember there will be no laundry in heaven.

Take a MOMENT to think about . . .

1. Do you have a song that takes you back to another time every time you hear it? How does it make you feel?
2. Is there anything in your past God wants you to let go of? How can you move forward without holding on to the past?

Dear Lord, Thank You for forgiving me for my past mistakes and for not holding those mistakes against me. You never let me fall too far away from You, I see that now. Thank You for my "foxhole" buddies. I'm glad they are the specific crew You decided to unite me with and I ask that You keep them out of the line of fire of the enemy today and every day. Teach me how to pray for them and how to battle when necessary. Teach me how to fight in love. Amen.

I Try to Be a Good Wife

"A wife of noble character who can find?
She is worth far more than rubies. Her husband
has full confidence in her and lacks nothing
of value. She brings him good, not harm, all the
days of her life." ~ Proverbs 31:10–12 (NIV)

I'm not one to brag on my domestic skills; I'm not like my mother. She knows how to make a fabulous hot meal and keep a tidy house with no effort whatsoever. I didn't inherit those skills. I was too busy doing ballet, tap, and jazz to learn to cook. When I dated Ron, I made sure he knew what he was getting himself into. My other friends make dinner for their husbands all the time. I tell them, "Listen, I've lowered Ron's expectations so much that every time I fry an egg he gets excited. Learn from the master." But sometimes I try to go the extra mile for my husband because I'm just that cool.

Marriage has been a trial. They didn't tell me in pre-marital counseling sessions that there would be a man in my house trying to steal my closet space and that I would sometimes be called upon to feed him. We are both come-dians and work from home. Every day we wake up and say, "Um . . . don't you have somewhere you need to be?" Early in our marriage, when I traveled, I tried to be a good wife by reading cookbooks. I thought I would make an effort and cook for him.

Ron enjoys the fine art of eating and sleeping. He's really good at it. On one of my first attempts, I decided to try one of my mom's easier recipes that I had seen her make a thousand times. It's called Broccoli Cheese Corn Bread. It's a southern favorite. All you need is corn bread mix from the box, cheese, and broccoli. I thought this would be a snap, and I was doing fine until about midway through I realized I was not using the Cheese Corn Bread mix but the Blueberry Corn Bread mix. I didn't think it would matter that much. Maybe he would enjoy the extra fruity flavors? I just picked some of the blueberries out and kept cooking.

I made the rest of the recipe and served it to him with a big smile. I looked cute in my pink apron. I saw him bite into the corn bread experiment and almost choke. Truth be told it was disgusting. If we had a dog, I wouldn't have fed this purple and green mess to him. The dog would probably have died. Ron did his best to be polite and swallow. Inside I was laughing but I wanted to see how long it would take him to comment on how bad my cooking was. He didn't say a word. He ate the whole thing. He only put two bites in his napkin when he thought I wasn't looking. It was amazing. Later that night I confessed that I knew it was horrific and asked him why he didn't tell me how bad it was. He said, "Kerri, beggars can't be choosers and food is food. I just thought it can't get much worse than this so I wanted to encourage you to keep trying. And with your lack of cooking skills, I'm bound to lose some weight. So overall, this setup is a win-win for me!"

I love that attitude and it hasn't changed. If I make any effort to cook for him, he's eternally grateful. Now, I can't say the same for the other two rug rats at my kitchen table, but at least I know there is one person in my home that will always enjoy my cooking.

Take a MOMENT to think about . . .

1. Name one positive quality about your spouse. Is he really grateful for you? Is he a positive thinker?

2. How can you show him you appreciate him today?

3. What is his love language and when is the last time you used it?

Dear Lord, When I think about my husband, please allow me to remember all his good qualities and attitudes. When things are rocky between us, bring to mind the positive moments in our marriage so I can get my head on straight and stop being so angry and judgmental. Amen.

The Great Chicken Standoff

"Children, you belong to the Lord, and you do the right thing when you obey your parents." ~ Ephesians 6:1 (CEV)

It started like any other night. Ron was working so I just had to make dinner for my two darlings and get them to bed. I had tried this new chicken recipe, where you actually take a raw chicken and bake it. My other recipes involved buying a chicken from Costco.

I had slaved over this meal, using vegetables and lemons, creating a sauce to cover it. I unveiled my creation to the girls and immediately realized that the chicken was pink on the inside. I took out the pieces I had planned to serve and placed them in the microwave. It occurred to me that microwaving food takes out the nutrients, but I prayed for God to do a "nutrient" miracle. I placed the chicken on Lucy's plate and after she took one bite, she screamed, "Ewwwww!"

I found some leftover mac and cheese and heated it up in the plastic container, knowing that it's unhealthy to do so. I prayed to God to spare us from the "toxin disease." Ruby started ferociously eating the chicken without her fork like some wild animal. I realized that I had forgotten to put on her bib so that should make for some interesting laundry stains. I then started yelling at Lucy to "sit like a lady" at the table and eat her meal. I know that I am no role model, as I stood by the sink doing the dishes, eating a piece of bread covered in peanut butter, which I recently read causes fungus. I reached for probiotic pills to combat the peanut butter.

Lucy chimes in, asking me if we can have "hot chocolate for dessert." I say yes as long as she finishes her dinner. She says, "I'm full!" I say, "Fine, then no hot chocolate!" She says, "I only have room for liquid!" I immediately start my usual dinner negotiation. "Well, if you eat three carrots and two more bites of chicken you can be done." She says, "I want fresh carrots, not the ones in water!" The water she's referring to is the homemade sauce that I will never make again. I just want her to eat veggies so I get out fresh/raw carrots and she shoves them and a piece of chicken in her mouth. I appreciate her excitement to eat my cooking but realize she's just trying to get it over with. As for negotiations, I feel I won.

I get the edamame out of the fridge and start throwing it on the baby's plate to make her eat something green. She is covered head to toe with mac and cheese. I begin wiping the floor. I look up and Lucy is rolling around in the middle of the kitchen floor like she's on fire. She's got her mouth closed but she's motioning like she's eaten poison and must spit it out. I have seen this tactic before where the child makes herself gag and therefore doesn't ingest my food. Not this time. I calmly said, "Fine, spit it out and see what happens!" (sounding like Dirty Harry-Make My Day).

She manages to "choke it" down and I end up making the hot chocolate. After all of this madness, this kid still gets hot chocolate? How does she do that? I don't want her to dip her fingers in the Cool Whip, but she bats her eyes and says, "Come on . . . be a cool mom, just this once?" Of course we both dip our fingers in the creamy contents and pig out.

Thinking back on that kid and his bread and fish . . . I bet he wished he had handed Jesus some candy instead!

Take a MOMENT to think about . . .

1. What are mealtimes like in your family? Do you have any strategies that work to get kids to eat quietly? (If so, please find me on Facebook and message me! I want to know!)

2. Do you often argue and try to negotiate with your heavenly Father? What can you do to release some of those traits that keep you from Him?

Dear Lord, Thank You for providing for my family and me. Thank You for giving me patience for my children but for also having patience with me. Amen.

Top Five Resolutions a Mom Should Never Break

1. Say something nice to your spouse every day. It may be "nice shirt" because that's all you can muster but it will change your marriage.

2. Be nice to people? Sound easy? Only if you are a saint. But remember the next time you're dealing with a customer service debacle or in the long check-out line that these employees are people too with feelings. Just picture your pastor standing next to you and act accordingly.

3. Decrease your social media time and replace it with reading your Bible. You can do it. Get the Bible app on your phone and make a vow that this is the first app you open in the morning. It's better than any "comments" on your wall.

4. Pray with your family. Don't stress out if it's not as much as you think it should be. Just make an effort to pray with them when it comes to mind. It's setting an example to your kids that prayer is important outside of church and it will become a habit if you stick to it.

5. Smile at your kids. Don't let them grow up thinking Mommy never laughed. Remember how much you wanted them before they arrived and how much you WILL miss them when they're gone. Whatever it takes, let them see you laugh once a day because it will leave a lasting impression on their hearts.

My Marital Bed Is Broken

"An endless dripping on a rainy day and a nagging wife are alike." ~ Proverbs 27:15

At the beginning of our marriage, I pulled another scheme and somehow ended up with a broken marriage bed. Let me explain. When we got married, we were given a decent amount of money so we decided to use it to purchase a new mattress. After looking at several different types, we decided on the Sleep Number mattress. We had a problem though. They cost $2,500 and we were a bit short. We agreed to save and six months later I announced to Ron that we now had the funds and I would go ahead and get us our new Sleep Number Bed.

Here is where things got messy. I went online and stumbled upon a similar type of bed that had everything the Sleep Number Bed advertised. It was called the Sleep Mumber and it really looked the exact same! And the best part was that this bed only cost $1,200, not the $2,500. I thought, "What a steal!" So, I called up Luanne in their customer service and ordered our new bed. It was scheduled to be delivered the next day.

Sure enough, the next day I answered the door to two huge guys standing at the top of my second floor apartment who looked like they just got off parole. Just the guys. The mattresses were still in their truck! When they saw my stairs, they came up with some excuse that it wouldn't fit through my door. One of the guys said, "Sign here!" and then he told me to come out to their truck. Here I was, standing in the back of this unlabeled truck, which looked like it had just come from some back alley, thinking how in the world was I going to get this up my stairs, by myself! I told him that I would help but neither of them was leaving until I got my bed. So after two phone calls to their manager, they got the boxes up my stairs. Then I said to them, "Okay, get started!" They both looked at me as if I was insane. "Uh ma'am, we're just the delivery company. We don't install them." Then they bolted out my door as if they saw a cop.

Here I was, stuck with huge boxes in my bedroom and no bed. I thought to myself, "I can do this myself," so I got out a kitchen knife and started cutting away through all the boxes. It contained a bunch of tubes, plastic bubbles, and things that scared me. How was this mess going to provide me with those hours of heavenly sleep like Luanne promised? I spent the next two hours trying to make heads or tails of the whole thing. I don't read directions, so I just tried to make it up as I went along.

That evening Ron comes home and sees me whimpering, surrounded by hundreds of bed parts. He had no idea what I had done. I knew I had to sweet talk my way out of this situation so I yelled, "Surprise Honey! Our Sleep Number Bed is here!" He wasn't buying it because he knew good and well that they would have assembled it. He then exclaimed, "Kerrrrrrrrrriiiii . . . What have you done?" Then the waterworks came and I went into my sob story of trying to do something nice for my husband by surprising him with a cost-efficient alternative. I told him all about the Sleep Mumber and its high customer rating. (Okay, I made that part up!) I was hoping we'd both giggle together and order pizza, but he knew I had gotten some knock off blow-up, ghetto version of the real thing. He also knew there was no return policy!

My Marital Bed Is Broken

We did finally get the bed put together, but Ron's side of the bed started to sag. It was slow at first with it kind of leaking air in the middle of the night. So night after night he would pump up his side of the bed to extra firm and awaken the next morning with the splinters from the wooden posts in his back. He'd get crankier each day. I, of course, told him he had two options: (1) Fix the thing, or (2) Sleep on the couch. I think I was secretly voting for option two because I'd get more snore-free nights.

Leave it to some ingenuity, but Ron did save the day. Well, actually it was the duct tape. Ron climbed under the bed and taped up the hole in the air hose with duct tape and it worked like a charm. We had no more leaks! Whoever says duct tape can't save a marriage obviously hasn't tried hard enough. That was almost nine years ago and the thing is still hanging in there. And so is my marriage. I guess that mattress is very symbolic of marriage. You might have some leaks, and sometimes things start to sag, but with God and duct tape anything can be fixed!

Take a MOMENT to think about . . .

1. Have you ever bought something that caused a riff in your marriage? How did you work it out?

2. How has Christ's love and forgiveness for you taught you how to forgive others?

Lord, Thank You for an understanding and loving spouse. Please help me to be more Christlike and understanding to him and to others. Thank You for loving me with all of my faults and helping me to be a better wife and mother. Amen.

Let Us Eat Cake (and anything else we want)

Therefore, whether you eat or drink, or whatever you do, do everything for God's glory. ~ 1 Corinthians 10:31

I say let every woman decide for herself, within reason of course, what she will or will not eat. I'm sick of others telling me, a grown woman, what I should eat. My mother raised me right. We ate homemade lasagna from the orange box (Stouffers) and homemade broccoli and cheese from the Green Giant. I turned out okay.

I'm worried about the kids that eat only organic or just healthy food. Hear me out. If you don't give your child chocolate and he or she doesn't know the delectable taste of frosted cake icing or ice cream, what do you think is going to happen when you drop them off at their friend's birthday party when they're four? Do you think all of the other kids in the neighborhood are serving organic carob cake with no additives? No way! The birthday kid's mom got out the Duncan Hines cake mix and frosted it for all the little kiddies to go home in a sugar-induced coma. That's what American moms do. If it's that organic kid's first time to taste sugar, they will end up on the ceiling.

I get this love for food from my childhood. We were the champion buffet eating family. If it said All You Can Eat, we were there. Of course there were rules set in place by my father, such as:

1. Salad is for sissies and hippies. It's wasted space in your stomach and on your plate.

2. Go directly for the crab legs or shrimp if they have them to really get your money's worth.

3. Always get four or more desserts. It's free and that way you can at least get a taste of them all.

4. Don't waste your calories on those fancy cheese cubes and crackers. It's a ploy to divert your attention from the prime rib carving station or the baked ham.

5. If you think you're full, get one more plate of food. Mom has a plastic bag in her purse and we can take home your leftovers.

6. Condiments in packets are meant to be taken from your table. They can be used with the leftovers that mom has in her purse.

7. Try to eat at the buffet before 5:00 p.m. so that you can get the Early Bird Special.

8. Although gluttony is a sin, God understands and He will forgive you since this is in fact an All You Can Eat buffet.

9. Pace yourself because they can't kick you out. Legally they can't. Stay for four hours . . . be free people! Have your crab legs and eat them too!

10. Never partake of the chocolate fountain. It may look inviting, but they found a "finger" in there last week!

All joking aside, I'm quite aware of people that go hungry each and every day and definitely want to teach my children the importance of good nutrition. Scripture says "Whether you eat or drink, or whatever you do, do everything for God's glory." I think we should teach our children the importance of feeding the homeless and giving to those that are less fortunate. I certainly don't want to instill the bad habits of eating cocoa puff cereal for breakfast, lunch, and dinner into my daughter's brain until she's at least in college. Of course, then it's just cost efficient to eat cereal for all three meals a day, staying hyped up on sugar for those late night study sessions. So make it a tradition to not only hit the buffets but to also feed the homeless at your church or local shelters. Bring that carob cake if you must!

Take a MOMENT to think about . . .

1. What has God blessed you with that you can share with others, even if it's just food?

2. How can you instill values in your children that not only teach them the importance of helping others but also help them to grow spiritually?

Dear Lord, Thank You for the many blessings You have bestowed on me. Thank You for always providing for me and my family. Help me to always see that I need to be there for others. Amen.

Princess Mentality

"Therefore, as God's chosen people, holy and dearly loved, clothe yourselves with compassion, kindness, humility, gentleness and patience. Bear with each other and forgive one another if any of you has a grievance against someone. Forgive as the Lord forgave you."
~ *Colossians 3:12–13 (NIV)*

I was asked to speak at a women's conference titled "Princess Mentality—Becoming a Daughter of the King." The night before, my sweet husband Ron assured me the car would be gassed up, and everything was ready to go. That morning my alarm went off at 6:00 a.m., so I would be ready to be at my sound check at 7:45. I came out of our bedroom only to see Ron sprawled out on the floor asleep. "We gotta go!" I said. He didn't respond. I shook his shoulder and resorted to my "Mommy voice." "Ronald Andrew McGehee! You get up!" I shouted.

We goet to the car and I asked, "Where is all the stuff you were going to pack for me?" He replied sleepily, "What stuff? You asked me what?" I told him, "I asked you to pack my things last night and you said you would take care of it, remember?" He replied, "I must not have heard you. I was tired." My mind started racing. The blood was rushing to the veins in my forehead and there was no stopping the explosion that was about to happen.

I started raving about how disappointed I was. The next thing you know we're having it out with each other as we hurriedly pack the car and head down the road to give all these women spiritual enlightenment. I knew I should calm down, but I didn't know if it was physically possible.

I was yelling at Ron in the car. "Now look what you've done. I'm all angry and my show is going to suck! Cause God won't bless it! We won't sell anything to help pay our expenses because you made me mad and made me sin!" He said, "Kerri, you really need to re-think about the God we serve. He's not vindictive the way you're portraying Him." He was right, which made me even madder.

Around 7:38, Ron slowly pulls our car over to the side of the freeway and mutters, "Um . . . we're out of gas." I was in so much shock I didn't even know how to respond. I knew we were definitely going to be late to my sound check and also I remembered he promised to gas up the car. Those two things were making the veins in my head pulsate fiercely again.

The next thing you know I see Ron with a gas can literally running through traffic. We should have been on "The Amazing Race." Ron gets back and I'm just about to lose my mind and my cell phone rings. I put on my fake phone voice and say to my client, "Oh Judy, I'll be there in a jiff!" I hung up and said, "Now what do you have to say for yourself? Huh?" He said, "Can I pray for you?" I was thinking, *he's pulling that card? Oh no he didn't!* I answered, "Well, you can pray, but I'm so mad, I'm not closing my eyes! And you better pray something good cause I have to be 'Super Christian' in thirty minutes in front of 450 women!"

I arrived at the conference and I had about five minutes to prepare. I prayed, "God, I know I sucked this morning, but I need you right now! Please forgive me and help me do some good for these ladies." All I could hear in my heart was the words, "Tell them about your morning!"

I went on stage and started off my talk with, "Well my husband forgot to put gas in our car this morning and when we ran out of gas, I showed him my 'real princess mentality.'" They laughed. I continued. "Ya know? I couldn't come before you today without letting you know how hard it was for me to even get here!" I went on to share with these women that we're never going to stop having crazy mornings. We will continue to fall down and make idiots of ourselves in front of others and behind closed doors. I told them I think the best gift we can give each other and ourselves is to take our "Perfect Christian" masks off and get real.

God totally blessed me that morning as I shared from my own struggles to appear "perfect." It really struck a chord. After my session, I sold every single book I brought. As if that wasn't great enough. God ordained 450 women to come up to Ron individually and say, "Hey! So you're the guy who ran out of gas? Nice work, honey!" God's got my back.

Take a MOMENT to think about . . .

1. Can you remember a time when someone made you so mad and you did not
   respond with any grace?
2. How would you do it differently if you
   could?

Dear Lord, Thank You for loving me unconditionally and for forgiving me every single time I screw up. Please remind me that Your grace never runs out for me and help me to extend that grace to others. Amen.

Five Things Husbands Must Know Living with a Pregnant Wife

1. Your wife is losing her mind.

Calm down. I did not use the word "crazy." I even put it in quotes to protect me. Did you read *Flowers for Algernon*? It's the story of a man who is really dimwitted. They give him a drug and he becomes super smart. The drug wears off and he slides back down to his dimwittedness. Your pregnant wife is experiencing that last part.

You see women have a supercomputer for a brain. They can do ten million things at once. Most of that is used for shopping, gossip, and Facebook posts. Now they have a leach in their system. And that leach is taking all the nutrients from Mommy's supercomputer. Slowly Mommy's intellect is being diminished down to the level of a worm.

Pick up the slack and let your wife take it easy. Your wife's supercomputer will come back online. Now you have a possible name for your unborn child, Algernon.

2. You didn't see nuthin'!

In that movie *Mr. & Mrs. Smith*, Angelina Jolie's character had all these gadgets hidden throughout the house ready for an emergency. In your house, those gadgets are called chocolate. You may come across a secret stash, but do not acknowledge it. Late at night you may find your wife's chocolate covered face ransacking the cupboards. Say nothing and live. Remember the saying, "Snitches wind up in ditches."

Your wife will be dealing with a lot of changes. Hidden chocolate is no big deal. Maybe even contribute to her stash. "Pssstt, sea salt and dark chocolate inside the bread box." And if you don't "see" her, maybe she doesn't see those "sympathy" chili dogs.

3. You are the bad guy.

I don't mean everything's your fault . . . but it could be. When news gets out that you're expecting, craziness will ensue! Giggly voicemails will turn into people trying to rub your wife's belly for good luck. You must be there to stop it. A maniac running toward your wife is pretty straight forward, but the subtleties of friends and family are tricky. Your wife may be tired, achy, or doesn't want to see anyone. She doesn't tell them, you do. You take the blame and let everyone know your wife can't see them. You are the bad guy. Maybe now for the first time. This role will extend after your child is born, when people will try to take her picture after thirty-six hours of labor, no shower, and no make-up. If that photo makes it to the Internet, your child will most definitely be fatherless. You're just like Batman. You're thought to be a villain, but you are actually the hero protecting the one you love. Also, instead of a utility belt you are wearing a fanny pack.

4. Stretch marks—get ready, set, go!

As your wife's body prepares for giving birth, some remodeling will be going on. Much of that deals with an increase in square footage. Yes, I am trying to tactfully say that your wife will be getting larger. Before anyone starts swinging punches, this is a fact and I heard it on *Dr. Oz.* These changes will concern your wife. Fortunately there are many remedies available. Just about any area that is having a growth spurt can use cocoa butter rubbed liberally at least once a day. (You may want to ask first.)

Some pregnant ladies experience swollen feet or restless leg syndrome. Both mean massaging the feet and calves are a must. I read on a website we'll call IHOPEMYGUYFRIENDSNEVERFINDOUT.COM that peppermint oil is very effective. When rubbing the feet, do not rub the heal or Achilles tendon. This has been known to induce labor. And you don't want your guest to arrive until you've figured out how to put the crib together.

Stretch marks don't matter to men. We just want our wives to feel as comfortable as possible. So if they want you to rub swamp moss on their knees to make them shiny, do it. They are worth it and more.

5. All you need is love.

Mistakes made, moods misread, noses punched. With a pregnant wife, more than five things are needed to survive pregnancy. That's why everything must be done marinated in love. Wives ask. Husbands try. Frustration grows.

As a child playing on walkie-talkies, when I couldn't talk to my brother, I would change channels to get better reception. Sometimes he would change channels too. This would have us on incompatible frequencies. We always had a base channel. A channel we knew each other would eventually turn to so we could clearly talk. Love is your base channel. No matter what could be misconstrued or block your channels of communication, you both can always turn to love and be able to speak clearly with one another.

Heartaches and Battles

The LORD is close to the brokenhearted and saves those who are crushed in spirit. ~ Psalm 34:18 *(NIV)*

It's 3:10 in the morning and I can't sleep. Today was Christmas and my friend died. He had cancer and he said to me, "I'm not gonna die from this!" Everyone believed him. He was young, a husband and father. Everyone prayed in total faith and knew he was going to win this battle. My friend's mom, who is like family to me, was put on hospice today and they have said she has only days to live. I have another friend whose son was killed in a car accident Christmas week. I don't have words. I don't know if I even have prayers. I don't understand this world at all. I know today of all days is supposed to be about joy and celebration, but my faith is being tested. My heart is breaking, as I check on my own two girls knowing that there are parents right at this moment mourning the loss of their children and spouses who have lost their loves. These are good people, people who read the Bible and believed in Christ, yet death still came. How am I supposed to keep my faith for what I believe when others that are much stronger than I have lost their own battle?

Do you have someone you love who is sick, or something in your life that is testing your faith. If so, I have written this prayer for all of us:

Hear my prayer, oh Lord. Help me to believe. I dare not ask that You grant me understanding because until I meet You face-to-face Lord, I will not understand Your ways with my tiny earthly brain. I know You are sovereign and I know Your heart is every bit as sad as mine tonight for all that You see in the world; death, dying, rejection of Your Son. This is just one of those moments where I have to admit I wish there was a formula for faith. One plus one equals two. It says in Your Word, Father God, that our prayers will be answered. We all pray that our loved ones will be spared death's early grip? Who am I to question You? Is it wrong? I know You told Job not to question Your ways, but David often questioned You in the book of Psalms when he cried out to You in anguish and You called him a man after Your own heart. I am in anguish, God. As a mother, I need to believe in miracles. As a daughter and a student of Your Word, I need to still have hope in healing, because if I don't, I don't know how I'll survive or raise kids in this fallen world. I have to believe You will still come through for me. I'm still fighting, still believing in these big things You've put on my heart. My children are a walking testimony of Your great power. You've told me to keep fighting for my children in prayer, supplication, and praise. I praise You even though I can't see the finish line.

Father, something inside of me screams to not entertain these thoughts. I don't have peace thinking about failure. I'm their mother and someone needs to rally for them. As they sleep so peacefully, I cannot think for a second about giving up. I fight knowing we will meet again someday. But Lord, I need Your comfort. Lord, I need Your strength. I cannot do this without You. Instead of curling up in a ball and quitting, I'm asking You to make me stronger than ever. Make me a better warrior for myself and those You've put on my heart to battle for. I will not give up. I will cling to Your promises despite what my earthly eyes can see. Another chapter of victory is just around the corner. I can feel it in my spirit and for that

I am thankful. Even as I pour out my heart to You, I can feel hope rising within me. It doesn't make sense that in the same moment I want to desperately weep, I also want to praise You for delivering my family from all the attacks against us. Help me to switch off my brain from earthly logic and allow You to minister to my heart and my soul because that is where You will meet me. That is where I can hear You best. My heart and my soul need You so badly. Speak to me, Lord. I am listening.

Take a MOMENT to think about . . .

1. When you are in your darkest time, do you allow the Lord an inroad to speak to you?

2. During the trials and tribulations of others, how can you help them see Christ in you?

Dear Lord, Thank You for hearing our prayers. Thank You for answered and unanswered prayers, as we know You have a plan and purpose for all things, even if we cannot see what that is. Amen.

I'm Not Fat, I'm Pregnant

"Charm is deceptive, and beauty is fleeting; but a woman who fears the LORD is to be praised." ~ Proverbs 31:30 (NIV)

If you haven't seen the movie *Moms' Night Out*, you have to see it. Angela Johnson is in it and is wonderful! This is the story of the night we met, when I was pregnant.

I started showing when I was about three minutes into the pregnancy. When I was three months pregnant, I was asked to perform for two nights at a Comedy Showcase in Hollywood.

I was feeling pretty good about myself until I see this tiny adorable girl of about twenty-three walk in. I couldn't even hate her because she was being nice to me and telling me how I had inspired her as a clean comic. So she's not only cute and thin, she's a clean comic too? It gets worse.

She proceeds to tell me she does Christian events. I thought I was the "hot chick" of the Christian comics. Now she wants to come steal my throne? I knew this day would come but who could prepare me. She had just moved to Los Angeles and now was up for a movie role with Forrest Whitaker. Academy award winner Forrest Whitaker!

The show started and I went out and did my act and was feeling pretty good about my pregnancy that nicely fit into my comedy routine. Then Angela comes out and kills it. My husband had to stop for doughnuts on the way home to calm my nerves. It worked for two minutes and then I was back to my monologue about how much skinnier Angela was than me. My husband finally had it and yelled, "You're pregnant silly!" I responded, "So she's prettier and hotter than me and you want her for your hot wife don't you?" He shoved a doughnut in my face and I fell asleep eating it.

I woke up the next morning bound and determined to be skinny again, which meant my size 4 skinny jeans. I grabbed those jeans and attempted to put them on. I thought of smearing Crisco oil on my belly, but I decided there had to be a better way. I had a "MacGyver" moment, so I took a pink rubber band and twirled it around the button on my jeans and looped it in the buttonhole to make a sort of bridge so the pants would not button but would be pulled together. Did this cut off my circulation? Yes! But more importantly, did I look good in those jeans? Yes! Breathing is overrated anyway.

Angela opened the show that next day with another sassy performance. I decided we could be friends . . . *after* the baby came. Finally, it was my turn. I was getting big laughs and I felt good. I was back into my routine and I decided to go for my big Pilates joke, which required some special physical comedy moves. The big finale was a kick in the air. I told the punch line and as my leg was rising in the air all I could hear was a smack and pop. Then I see the rubber band around the button of my jeans fly off into the air and onto the floor in front of me. It was a huge bright pink thing, and when it went flying, it appeared to come from my belly button. I should also mention that my jeans quickly started to slide down my thighs because my huge pot pregnant belly was now protruding in a way that no one could ignore. I looked like a can of Pillsbury dough that was just opened and the dough started spreading everywhere. I had a mic in one hand and there was no way the other hand was going to be able to save my jeans from falling down (which would have quickly made this an R-rated show).

I thought to myself, *Kerri, you're pregnant and you've got to face it. You're also a comedian and you can use this situation to your advantage.* I announced to the audience, "Oh, if you didn't notice, I'm not fat, I'm just pregnant! Yeah, that's what happens when you don't have cable TV!" They applauded. I triumphantly picked up my broken rubber band and waddled off the stage, triumphant.

As I look back on that night, two kids later, I have to laugh. I also have to admit I still have that pair of skinny jeans in my closet. They are in the way waaaaaaaaaaay back. But I keep them as a reminder that I still have "goals" and throwing them away would be admitting defeat. I also have chocolate hidden in my closet so that is probably hindering my goal in some fashion.

I don't regret being pregnant for a second. I know God created me with this body to give life into this world. He did not create skinny jeans. Those are from Satan. We've all had crazy pregnancy moments and it's all part of the "gig" of motherhood. And all in all, pregnancy was pretty amazing. Just think of how creative God is to allow us to carry a real live human life for nine months! I also know God is just up there laughing thinking, *Mama, You Ain't Seen Nothin' Yet!*

Take a MOMENT to think about . . .

1. What has motherhood taught you? How does that compare to God's love for you?

2. Does laughter play an important part in your parenting; an important part of your marriage? Why or why not?

Dear Lord, Help me to laugh, even when things get bad. Thank You for allowing me the privilege to carry Your children into this world. I'm even thankful for the battle scars I have to prove it. Amen.

Where Will We Be Standing?

"Blessed are those who are persecuted for righteousness' sake, for theirs is the kingdom of heaven." ~ Matthew 5:10 (ESV)

I know we moms want to set a good example for our kids. Although I know I have failed miserably millions of times, I want them to look up to me and the life I have lived. I was thinking about a time in my life when I just starting out in my acting career. I was playing the characters with scripts that were already written for me. After paying my dues, I created my own stand-up comedy act and was free to say things that I was passionate about. I got the control we Type-A women love.

One night I was performing at a famous Hollywood comedy club with other female comics who were doing disgusting sexual jokes. All I could do was to hope for the best. People loved my jokes and the fact that I said things like "Well, we Christians are hot right now! We're the new Kabala!" I knew I had to continue being unafraid of my beliefs and of course be good at my craft.

There was a TV producer in the audience who stopped me after that show. He said he wanted to meet with me about some possible TV opportunities based on my comedy act about my life as a "Good Girl." He was really intrigued and thought it would be a refreshing concept for a sitcom, such as a modern day *Mary Tyler Moore*. We had a few meetings and he was really excited about working with me. I was really new to the comedy scene, but I knew from experience that TV and film opportunities are a big deal.

One night this producer arranged a showcase at the largest comedy club in Los Angeles for a huge Hollywood manager to see me. I remember being so nervous that night. The guy working the box office was a friend of mine and fellow comic. He saw that I was nervous and did the strangest thing. He shut down the ticket booth and reached over and prayed with me. No one had ever done that in public before. It was sweet.

I went on to have a good show; the response was positive. The producer called and the first thing he said was,

"You really played that whole God card hard, huh?" I didn't know what he meant. He continued, "Ya know you mentioned God several times on stage and that's really going to pigeonhole you with those people." "What people?" I asked. "You know, those Christians. If you want to make it big in this town, you have to manipulate your faith and not be so open about it. I even saw you praying before the show. That's a bad move if you want to be successful." I was in shock. I felt like I was literally being punched in the gut. I didn't know how to handle it.

During my prayer and Bible study, I found Matthew 5:10, "Blessed are those who are persecuted for righteousness' sake, for theirs is the kingdom of heaven." I thought "Wow! This is really happening and it hurts, but I'm honored to stand up for Jesus for the first time in my life." I called the producer and politely witnessed to him about how my faith was way more important than anything he or Hollywood had to offer. I knew I trusted God. He would give me all the TV and movie deals in His perfect timing. I told the producer that when I do see God that I WANT to be pigeonholed with my people, the Christians.

I have been blessed with so many more opportunities than I could ever ask for. I have appeared on *The Tonight Show* and *Comedy Central* to name a few. I've gotten to be on *Showbiz Tonight* because I was a Christian! And do you remember that guy in the ticket booth? Well, I married him! See? God's good like that! I hope that by leading by example my kids will see that every time I have done what God has asked me to do, He has never let me down. It is my desire to show them that I always put God first in my life and that prayer really does work.

Take a MOMENT to think about . . .

1. Can you think of a time when you were persecuted for your faith? Share it with your children and use it as a learning moment.
2. How can you teach your children to stand strong for their faith? Discuss with them the importance of witnessing for Christ, even when it's difficult.

God, Thank You for always having my back. Thank You for giving me the courage to stand up for You, even when it's hard. Help me to lead my children by example and live a life they can be proud of. Amen.

Slow Dance

*"I will be with you when you pass through the waters, and
when you pass through the rivers, they will not overwhelm
you. You will not be scorched when you walk through the
fire, and the flame will not burn you." ~ Isaiah 43:2*

Okay, here's a crazy story. As I was writing another
devotion for this book, I heard my three-year-old crying
out to me from her bedroom. It's 9:30 p.m. I stopped
writing to check on her and she was standing up in her
crib with her arms wide open waiting for me to pick her
up. There was praise CD playing in her dimly lit room
while her older sister lay fast asleep. Ruby didn't want to
sleep, she wanted me to hold her and dance.

Ruby's nickname is "Party in the Crib" because she
never wants to sleep. She will just sing to herself and jump

around all night until she passes out. We literally can't put her in a regular bed yet because she'd bounce out in three seconds. Even though she is three, since she's my second child, I do whatever I can to keep her "my baby." She's also petite so I like to pretend I can still cradle her even though she hates it! She wants to be free. When she does want to be held, even for a second, I'm there. I'll take it when I can get it. The older they get, the cuddles seem so fleeting.

She looks at me and says, "Up Mama?" So I pick her up and hold her tight in my arms. I smelled her hair and instantly had a flashback of me listening to this same worship CD while as an infant she laid in the Neo-Natal Intensive Care unit at UCLA hospital. I wasn't allowed to dance with her or free her from all of the wires and machines that were literally keeping her alive. We were practically living in the hospital, and my emotions were on autopilot. I knew if I played any kind of Christian music, I would lose my mind and might not recover.

One day, while home resting, I cried out to God and turned on this very CD. I immediately hit the floor sobbing. I cried out to Him and as my tears hit the wet carpet, I was moved to pray. Those prayers helped me to fight for my daughter. I believed that I could trust God in this very scary situation. I brought the music to her crib in the hospital and had it playing twenty-four-hours a day. She needed her mama to be strong and I wasn't going to let her down. The doctors said that Ruby had several incurable health problems that would require her to have oxygen and medications for years to come. They also said she might require leg braces or a walker to help her walk, but I asked for healing. I stood on God's promises and trusted in Him, praising Him. At first, I didn't see why I should praise Him, but I praised Him anyway. I praised Him from the floor and that was okay.

And as I held my healthy, bobbing, beautiful, singing Ruby Joy, we danced. The lyrics kept repeating, "You're beautiful to me. You're so beautiful." I sang it to my daughter but I knew in my heart God had me come into that room so He could sing it to me, "My daughter Kerri, you're beautiful, so beautiful to Me." God was calling me to have a moment with Him in that room. I'm glad I listened. I would have missed one of the best slow dances I've had in a long time if I had been too busy.

You never knew how much your life would change when you became a wife and a mother. I'm sure in the beginning you think about the possible loss of freedom, but look how fulfilled your life is because you trusted Him. I'm sure like me you have learned so much and can actually say you are thankful for the challenges that you have faced with your husband and children. I known it might sound crazy, but it's because of those challenges that you are better equipped to parent them for future trials. Just know that you can trust God and that He is always in your corner for whatever fight you might have. He will never EVER let you go it alone.

Take a MOMENT to think about . . .

1. Are you going through a "pass through the waters" moment right now, where you can't see the outcome? Have you in the past? How did you get through them and what have you learned?

2. What has God used to get your attention? Music? His Word?

Dear Father God, Thank You for allowing me to experience moments with my kids where You show me how infinite Your love is for me. Thank You for reminding me that I can "pass through the waters" and not drown, even when my tears seem to overtake me. You are my Strong Tower. You are my Deliverer. Thank You! Thank You! Amen.

Rebel with a Coke

"His divine power has given us everything required for life and godliness through the knowledge of Him who called us by His own glory and goodness." ~ 2 Peter 1:3

Somewhere in mid-November I took a friend's advice on dieting during the holidays. She said proudly, "See you in Jan Suckers!" I knew exactly what she meant. I had been dieting and working out diligently because my big 4-0 was this year and I wanted to fit into some slinky dress. So I did everything that was required to fit into "the dress" and then blew it all at my Willie Wonka birthday extravaganza. I'd been avoiding sugar, soda, bread, and pasta until my party. Then the next morning we went out for birthday brunch and I munched gloriously on French toast and fried chicken. After all, it was still my birthday weekend. Then Thanksgiving just kind of snuck up on me. Not only was I off the wagon, it had pulled over and there was no driver in sight. I knew I was in trouble when I went to a Black Friday sale at Loeman's and there were communal dressing rooms. At first I was freaked out by my ever expanding curves in fluorescent non-forgiving lighting. But as I looked around the room at the other thirty or so women cramming themselves into tight jeans, I realized I measured up just fine. So the wagon permanently parked for the rest of 2013.

By late December, I was at my parents' home, which is a bed of culinary sin. I decided to eat whatever I wanted, whenever I wanted, with the grand plan of getting a treadmill on January 1. It's not like I didn't have a plan. So what if I have been drinking sodas, eating candy bars and peppermint bark, and leading a life of freedom. I knew it was not good for me, but in the words of the Country music legend Barbara Mandrell, "If lovin' you is wrong, I don't want to be right." I sang that to all the Christmas candy. I just felt like I was a junkie who had been on a binge but I knew there is an end in sight. I just wanted to see how far I could bottom out before I had to come back down to reality. It was amazing to go to a movie and get candy and popcorn and not judge myself. I was at a drug store and actually bought a Snickers Bar and a soda. I felt like such a rebel. I didn't want my kids to see me because I have preached to them that soda is from the Devil and candy gives you "mushy brain." I don't think they knew how far Mommy had fallen off the health wagon. But I sort of loved it.

Today I ask myself, was that a good decision? What would my dandelion tea drinking friends think? Is it okay to take occasional breaks from trying to eat organic so I don't die of starvation (joking, of course!)? I had big goals to make homemade meals and smoothies in January and stop eating frozen lasagna with my kids every week. Am I living a life as a wife and working mother that is so structured and repressed that I have to go off the deep end and eat like a college kid for weeks on end to feel freedom? Some people eat this way all the time and for me it was only a few weeks. So what if I'm wearing oversized clothing and borrowing my mom's Christmas sweaters. So what if I hadn't seen a scale in ages because I didn't want the accountability. Am I setting a bad example for my kids even if they don't know about it?

I felt like such a hypocrite. Did my mother do these types of things? Do I disregard the good care of the body God gave me? If my body is a temple, we're gonna need some deep cleaning soon cause it's clogged up with Coke and Oreos. I wonder what God thinks of all my 24/7 cheating. I don't have the answers but I guess as they say, "It's food for thought!"

Take a MOMENT to think about . . .
1. Have you ever gone off the health wagon completely? How did it feel?
2. What spurred your choice on? Did you get back on the wagon?

Dear God, I've been so stressed out and it's shown in my recent behavior. I know You're not judging me but You want me to take good care of myself. I need help getting back in balance and I don't even know how to start. Please show me some tangible ways. Amen.

Dirty

"Am I now trying to win the approval of human beings, or of God? Or am I trying to please people? If I were still trying to please people, I would not be a servant of Christ."
~ *Galatians 1:10 (NIV)*

If you asked me to describe parenting in one word, it would have to be *dirty*. I mean it, in the literal sense. I took my kids and one of their friends to the Farmer's Market the other day. By the time we had ordered our crepes and side dishes and found an outside table (in order to get some fresh air), the kids and I were gross. I really feel like there are not enough wet wipes in the world to clean up after me and my kids. This is not their fault. It's generational. My mom spills things, I spill things, and when you add kids it's just more spilled things. I really think about

70 percent of my human existence is spent cleaning. I don't think I have classic OCD unless you count the fact that I can't walk in my house without immediately wiping something or picking something up. Even if I'm on vacation, I'll start throwing things in bins before I will even go to the bathroom or sit down. Sound familiar? I think all moms have a touch of this disorder.

When it was just me I could manage it, but now there are little people and a grown man in my house, and there is no place else to go. The clutter or mess does not seem to take a toll on them the way it does me. I hear all the poems about "When the kids are gone, my house will be spotless. Each sock will have a match and I will be sad." I try to repeat that to myself when I'm cleaning Playdoh out of my carpet or wiping chocolate out of my three-year-olds hair AFTER I just bathed her.

I just feel dirty all the time. I wonder about other mothers. I have a friend that is a celebrity and she has kids. She is so pretty, and so put together and seemingly CLEAN all the time. I've never seen her in anything but a designer outfit and she even bakes yet still looks clean. Do you think celebrity moms have a nanny that follows them around and cleans each breadcrumb off their newly mopped floors as it falls? There are some moms that just seem so perfect and I wonder how I can even remain friends with them. It's like I'd love to find just one tiny, well huge, flaw in them so I could feel better about my situation. One time I'd love to go to my perfect friend's house, the one with the nine Christmas trees she personally decorated, and see piles of dirty laundry hidden in her bedroom. I'd love to see what she looks like with Mexican food smeared on her sweater or does she ever wear anything that doesn't match?

Maybe, maybe not, but why do I care so much? Why are we always comparing ourselves to others? And it seems to get worse when we become parents. It's like we're in some unspoken competition to have the most darling, well behaved, and clean family on the planet. I think some of the moms I'm "competing" with don't even know they're beating me. I need to stop. I need to slow down and wipe the enchilada sauce off my sweater and enjoy my life. My kids will never be this age again, ever. I will not get this moment back. I want to endeavor to embrace more moments instead of trying to "clean them up and survive them." So what if my kids don't get bathed tonight? Sponge Bob Square Pants is having a marathon and the chocolate pretzels won't eat themselves! I know I can't change these attitudes of comparing myself to others overnight. I didn't immediately become like this. It took years. But at least I still want to try. We should appreciate that about ourselves. God can change us, if we are willing to try to change. As I type this, my daughter is hanging on me wanting me to go play. I think Lucy and I are going to go downstairs and spend some quality time together, and I won't even wipe the mashed potatoes out of her hair until later. Hey, it's a start.

Take a MOMENT to think about . . .

1. Do you have MOM OCD when it comes to cleaning?
2. Are you merely surviving most moments with your kids or are you enjoying those precious moments?
3. What changes would you like to make in this area?

Dear God, I don't want to be stressed out about how I compare to others. It's a pattern that is not healthy and I need You to help me take steps to break it. Help me to appreciate each moment as it comes and break my "survival" mentality so I can have more fun with my family. Amen.

Bite Club

"Do not be anxious about anything, but in every situation, by prayer and petition, with thanksgiving, present your requests to God." ~ Philippians 4:6

There are certain clubs I never EVER intended to become a member of and one of them is "Bite Club." If you're a member and you're reading this, you feel my pain. Literally! My child was a predator. I didn't see this coming on the ultrasound. I mean we knew she was gifted from all the sonograms; we just didn't have a clue how that was going to play out in the forty-seven church day cares she's been "asked to leave." Can you believe they could kick out a one-year-old? We couldn't leave her in a church day care for more than seven minutes before we got the page to come pick her up. They'd say, "Perhaps she'd be more comfortable with you," which meant anywhere else but here!

You know when you drop your kid off and they give you a number, you are not listening to the sermon, you're watching the screen thinking, "Please don't call 232!" This type of event was not just a Sunday occurrence. Her biting happened all the time in all different situations. I tried everything, even the worst tactics. I even bit her back one time. She cried. I cried. Then she struck again the very next day. Obviously reasoning with a one-year-old on why "pulling hair is a better option because it doesn't leave a scar" doesn't work. She literally bit everyone and everything in sight.

Basically all the books said she would grow out of it. Gee, that's easy for them to say. They're not having panic attacks every time their kid got into a jumpy house with other victims, I mean kids. It got so bad that she even bit my hairdresser's cat. This was rock bottom . . . my hairdresser's cat?

We went through a period of isolation. I dropped out of baby class because she was literally scarring other children. My mom friends tried to comfort me, but unless they were in "Bite Club" they just didn't get it. I was scared that this problem would go on through adulthood. This was the hardest issue I had faced as a parent and the worst part of the battle was the feeling of complete helplessness. Now that she's six, I see that this time in her life was a valuable lesson God was teaching me. No, we can't change our children's behavior. They are going to do stupid things that hurt other people, hurt themselves, and yes hurt us. It's going to happen. It's what we do in the moment that is going to define our mental state of being. Having a biter was probably one millionth of the pain a mom feels whose child is on drugs or a kid that has walked away from the Lord and is in all sorts of bad situations. We cry, we pray, and we try our best not to have a nervous breakdown.

Having a child brought all of my control freak issues right to the surface. I had to get a handle on it early so I could survive the challenges yet to come. The truth is nothing I did made Lucy stop biting. She grew out of it. She learned to talk and the rest is history. I realized the biting was her way of expressing herself when she couldn't use words. Now when the teachers call me over after school and say Lucy had a temper tantrum and broke a toy, I just quietly say, "Did she bite anyone?" If the answer is no, it's not that big a problem. I know I am a member of the "Bite Club." I can survive anything. Plus biter kids are probably going to run a country someday. We moms just need to harness their powers for good, not evil.

God gave me this strong-spirited child as a gift. The gift is that she's breaking me down and helping me become a more resilient, more prayerful, more powerful person. I will thank her one day, but not till she's thirty. I don't want her head to get any bigger than it already is. She already thinks she can walk on water!

Take a MOMENT to think about . . .

1. Did you have any behaviors from your children that were mortifying that you thought would never end? How did you handle them? How can you learn from those moments for the next time something comes up?

2. Do you have friends or loved ones who are also going through different parenting moments that you can speak into? What can you do to help them through this difficult time?

God, Thank You for designing the perfect kids for me. You use them as a learning tool on a daily basis. Help me to learn from each mistake and situation so I can handle it better the next time a battle arises. I won't quit fighting. I just need to learn to use my tools better and sometimes fight on my knees with you. It's my best weapon. Amen.

Parties and Pinterest

"I praise you, for I am fearfully and wonderfully made.
Wonderful are your works; my soul knows it very well."
~ Psalm 139:14 (ESV)

Okay, so sue me. I'm not one of those fancy Pinterest moms who make organic cotton candy machines that spew out Scripture verses. I don't have Tupperware with matching lids and when I go on Pinterest for more than thirty seconds I get a severe stomach ache. Why? Because it brings up all my insecurities that not only am I not crafty, I had to repeat kindergarten because I couldn't cut a straight line. My vocabulary skills were off the chart, but I couldn't draw a circle! So every time I'm faced with seeing all the adorable things I could be making for my family, including food items with faces, I kinda want to throw up a little.

I have Pinterest friends and I attend their gatherings. I

marvel at their party platter creations shaped like Noah's ark and ooh and ahh over their new hand-stitched curtains with homemade lamb's wool from Uganda. I listen intently about their latest gluten free bread recipes that are delicious and also cure cellulite, fibromyalgia, and diabetes all at the same time!

My neighbor Anne puts Martha Stewart to shame. The first day that I met her she was baking her own birthday cake right from the pin page of Martha's Easter Bunny 3-D cakes. She invited us over and I brought my handmade chocolate peanut butter balls that actually came out looking more like blobs than balls. I placed my creation by her perfectly shaped realistic Bunny cake and said, "Well, here are its droppings!" She smiled and we've been friends ever since. She sent her kids to preschools that use only organic clay, stuck to schedules, and that were so expensive you had to give a kidney to get in. I sent my kids to a preschool where the drop off time was "whenever you feel like it" and my kids ate the play dough and seemed okay to me.

I recently attended one of Anne's "Ginger Bread Making Parties" with my daughter. Lucy has unfortunately inherited my skills for crafts. We were working as a team to build one of these monstrosities and all my "issues" from kindergarten surfaced. I kept sneaking bites of all the toppings under the table. I caught Lucy doing it a few times too!

Lucy got so mad her house wouldn't stand up, she ran to the side of the garage pouting. I didn't blame her. Our house was horrific, to be honest. Anne had everything (including the homemade sugar glue) perfectly laid out but did not include any instructions on how to make the darn things. I approached Lucy and I tried to comfort her. She wanted to leave. I knew this was a moment that would be important to her later. I wasn't going to let her quit because she wasn't succeeding at it. She also inherited my perfectionist quality that can be a gift, as well as a curse, depending on the day. I convinced her to join the table again by promising her we could eat all the toppings secretly. I grabbed Anne's crafty husband and said, "Danny, can you hook us up with a gingerbread house that stands please?" He immediately went to work. Lucy and I happily ate gumdrops and chocolate chips as we saw "our" gingerbread house come to life. We then decorated it with joy and took all the credit. It looked totally ghetto but we were very proud. I told her it was the best looking gingerbread house in the world and the other kids were staring at it because they were so jealous of our "modern abstract art" concept (we ate the roof).

Lucy learned a lesson that day; we may not be good at everything we try, but quitting is not an option. I learned the importance of nurturing my daughter's self-worth, even when she was not excelling. The house might not have looked like anyone else's house, yet she was proud of herself and that's what mattered.

We also learned that gum drops and sprinkles are a perfectly acceptable lunch (on special occasions), as long as we wash it down with some organic gluten free Pinterest freshly squeezed lemonade with lemons that come from Spain.

Take a MOMENT to think about . . .

1. Do you march to your own drummer in some areas? Does that make you insecure?

2. Do you find yourself comparing your skills with other moms? If so, why? Do you think it's a good thing to compare you and your family members against others? Does Christ do that to you?

3. What can you do to receive the acceptance of your heavenly Father for who He made you to be and who He made others to be?

Dear God, You always show me how to make lemonade out of my lemon situations. Thanks for giving me a creative, unique mind. I know I'm like no one else and that's the way You created me. Please allow me to raise my kids and appreciate how special and unique they are and encourage them to be their own person. Remind me that You don't make mistakes. Amen.

Play Dates and Park Days, Oh Joy!

But He said to me, "My grace is sufficient for you, for power is perfected in weakness." Therefore, I will most gladly boast all the more about my weaknesses, so that Christ's power may reside in me. – 2 Corinthians 12:9

I hate park dates. I may be emotionally scarred from my first biter child that took a bite out of other kids flesh on every playground. One time she bit a girl who started crying. I actually saw Lucy say, "Shhhh . . . You're pretty!" Yes, that was my kid. So, at the park I never got to sit down because I never knew when she would strike again.

Today I ventured to give it another try with both of my kids. I forgot that my sweet Ruby thinks she can fly because her sister said she could. She took an Evil Knievel leap off the slide, and I could not get there in time to catch her. She landed flat on her head and all the parents rushed over to her before I could. They almost called an ambulance and Child Protective Services. Ruby was bawling! I immediately called my husband. "Ron, you better get over here, right now. I'm miserable and having a horrible time." I think the next time I'll just stay at the park with the moms without the kids! Am I a bad mom? I don't seem to like things other moms do. I think finger painting at Mommy class is totally boring. Plus neither I nor my kids are particularly artistically inclined so it looks like a crime scene at our station.

All this kids' stuff was supposed to be fun, yet it gives me a headache. I'm anxious all the time and I want to be somewhere else. I don't share this with many people because I don't want to be judged. Do other moms feel this way when they're running, swinging on ropes, or hanging in trees? I feel like such a phony. It just seems whenever I'm out in public one of my kids is getting into serious trouble. What is wrong with me?

The last kids' party we attended was at the beach. They had all types of entertainment and activities in the sand, away from the water. I look over and just like the Pied Piper, Lucy is running full speed with ALL of the children following her yelling, "Get Lucy! Get Her!" She is heading directly for the ocean, but the other parents, not knowing *my* child, aren't concerned. I'm sure they were thinking that there was NO WAY she would actually get in the water. Well, I take off running like a bad movie chase scene yelling "Luuuuuccy! Stooooooop!" She was too far from me. The other parents quickly notice that she is not stopping and neither are her followers, THEIR kids! She heads into the ocean like *The Little Mermaid,* as do I. Now we are both soaking wet. There are kids and parents spread all over the beach like a scene from *Lost.* It was chaos. I dragged my soaking wet daughter out of the water and everyone was laughing.

Maybe you can relate because you have "that kid"! What do we do? Should I ask God to change me or change my kids? Maybe they'll take an interest in the Food Channel? Or is it possible I'm just supposed to sacrifice my time and enjoyment because that's part of the job? I love my kids more than I thought humanly possible and that's why Saturdays are spent sitting in the T-Ball bleachers, watching Lucy lay in the grass in the outfield, or hours on end at parks and playgrounds pretending to be having the time of my life. Wow, is this what my mom did? Was she faking it too? I gotta give her a call! Someday my kids will realize all I've done for them. It may not be until their forty but there WILL come a day! Right?

Take a MOMENT to think about . . .

1. Are there things that you do for your kids that you actually can't stand to do? How do you find the grace to do it?

2. As a mom, what would you ask God to change about you if you could change?

Dear God, I am always exhausted. All I want to do is take a bubble bath. Can you please give me an extra ounce of Your grace to get up tomorrow and do this all over again? If You would be so kind, can You give me more of a heart like Jesus to love my kids and forgive quickly when needed. Amen.

An Interview with a Six-Year-Old: How to Be a Great Mom

KERRI: How am I doing as your mommy?

LUCY: Better than good . . . the best. But sometimes you treat us like servants.

KERRI: What do you think makes a great mommy?

LUCY: That one is so hard because I know I love you and you can do anything. Just being a mom is the greatest present you can give me. Just spending time with me and having fun with me. God made you great just the way you are.

KERRI: Are you trying to get more candy out of me?

LUCY: I'm not, I'm serious. That's what I think.

KERRI: Do you want kids someday Lucy?

LUCY: I want to be single because I don't want to get married cause I don't want to kiss.

KERRI: Great answer! How old do you have to be to date?

LUCY: Thirty, but I don't really know cause I want to be single.

KERRI: If someone wants to be a mom, what advice would you give them?

LUCY: You can be anything when you grow up.

KERRI: How old do you have to be to be a mom?

LUCY: Um . . . you can be thirty . . . or forty, it depends.

KERRI: What's the best thing about being six?

LUCY: You really get a happy life.

KERRI: Do you think you'd be a good mom, Lucy?

LUCY: I don't want to, remember? I don't want to kiss anyone. Are you trying to trick me? Are you writing this in your book, Mommy? It's fine if you do.

KERRI: Lucy, do you have anything you want to share with my readers about me?

CRICKETS . . .

She's busy playing "single girl" in her new Barbie Dreamhouse, which is good because there are a couple of secrets I don't want her to give away . . .

Mom's Chapter Out

"Therefore everyone who hears these words of mine and puts them into practice is like a wise man who built his house on the rock. The rain came down, the streams rose, and the winds blew and beat against that house; yet it did not fall, because it had its foundation on the rock. But everyone who hears these words of mine and does not put them into practice is like a foolish man who built his house on sand. The rain came down, the streams rose, and the winds blew and beat against that house, and it fell with a great crash."
~ Matthew 7:24–27 (NIV)

Good evening, ladies (and a few gentlemen winning the right to watch football on Sundays). My name is Ron and I will be your substitute author for this devotion. Kerri sprung this on me at the last minute and went out with her girlfriends, leaving me to take care of the children and our household. Kerri says she wrote it down on the family calendar, wherever that is.

KERRI: "Ron, the girls both need a bath. They need to be in bed by 7:30 and that is after story time. Dinner needs to be heated up at—."

ME: "I got it, I got it. I can take care of the girls. Don't worry, you go have fun at your—."

The door slammed shut, a car peeled out of the driveway, and I swear I heard cackling.

So, here we go!

BATH TIME: This event can be very misleading by watching a child's shampoo commercial. The kids are always well behaved and put on the most adorable faces, while the shampoo in their eyes does not bring tears. Turn the camera on the parents, and you will see bathwater soaked clothes and plenty of tears of frustration. Our problem that evening wasn't that I let Lucy have bubbles but that I let her administer them. It wasn't until I heard Ruby, my three-year-old, giggling that I remembered she was in there at all. So not only did I bathe the girls, but I washed the floor, toilet, sink, walls, and ceiling, all at one time.

DINNER TIME: Once they were squeaky clean and in their pj's, it was time to eat. I open the fridge, grabbed the pan, and after fifteen minutes of changing the clock, turning on the timer, and figuring out if I'm baking or broiling, I finally got the oven going. I got sucked into a Dora story and learned that the monkey was changing his name because of his choice in footwear. I guess "Stilettos" would've made Dora the sidekick. I knew I needed to feed these kids something nutritious and quickly make it to bed. Yes, pizza, God's delivery system for yummy vegetables. Pizza dough (flour), sauce (tomatoes), cheese (milk) topped with nutritious vegetables. Oh, and I also learned that our smoke alarm works. Remember those squeaky clean kids from before? Well they're gone and replaced with mozzarella mouth and sauce hair. After a box and a half of wet wipes, the girls resemble something clean.

STORY TIME: It's so beautiful! They are hugging and giggling, me and each other. But it's important to remember that even the most beautiful plants, flowers, fish, bugs, etc., are also the most deadly on Earth. I go and get a book and see pajamas discarded and Ruby has decorated her stomach and legs with a marker. I now see why large corporations do not leave three-year-old employees under the care of their six-year-old supervisors. I tell Lucy to clean up while I basically give Ruby bath number three for the night. I tell the girls no story time. Lucy says, "But we have to do our devotion." She holds out a child's devotion book. I open it to its place holder to: "The Wise and Foolish Builders." As I read the devotion, I realize that this story is speaking more to me than the kids.

After the girls are asleep, I clean up the kitchen and see the notorious Family Calendar ingeniously hidden on the front of our refrigerator door. And sure enough, "Mom's Night Out" is clearly written for tonight. Tonight didn't exactly go as planned. I feel like the Foolish Man from the kids' devotion. My house went crash! The only difference between the Wise and Foolish Man is putting into practice what they heard. I know how to keep my house in order. I know how to take care of my girls, but I just need more practice. I write down several dates on the calendar marked "Dad's Night In." Time to put what I know into practice.

Take a MOMENT to think about . . .

1. Is there anything that is stopping or hindering you from hearing from the Lord?
2. What are some things you "know" but have not put into practice?

Dear Lord, Please help me hear Your words. Let me know them in my heart. And most of all please help me to put them into practice. I want to build a strong foundation for me and my family. Let me be wise. Amen.

Let It Go

"Come to me, all you who are weary and burdened, and I will give you rest." ~ Matthew 11:28 (NIV)

There's something about New Year's Day that makes me exhilarated. Yesterday was January 1 and I pranced into a bookstore and as I saw the shiny cookbooks, my adrenaline started pumping. I wanted to cook and learn to make organic vegan comfort food for my family. I also wanted to wear those cute new aprons. I made a vow that I was going to become *Julie & Julia* and cook everyday for the rest of my life. When I passed the craft section, I also decided I was going to take up knitting and origami while cooking my organic vegan comfort foods. I felt free. New Years Day makes me feel like cooking, crafting, and flying. I was Peter Pan! I decided that it was time to make the changes, which would require huge commitments.

The next day I woke up at 6:00 a.m. to screaming kids and quickly forgot all about those changes. I got out the Pop Tarts for breakfast. My kids ate Taco Bell and sea-weed snacks (Ron's Korean) for lunch. Tonight I think they're eating smoked turkey and canned veggies. As for my healthy eating, I've eaten four peanut butter balls and two chocolate candies, cashews, and sugar free soda. This is going swimmingly.

I spent the day on prayer conference calls, nursing a sick husband, praying for my backaches, writing this book, play dates for the kids, and answering e-mails. I went around my house and anointed it with oil and prayed over my sick husband. I started making more "To Do" lists. I listened to my daughters serenade us with the Disney theme song from *Frozen* thirteen times. I now have the lyrics "Let it go! Let it go!" replaying in my head.

So much for making commitments. I know the Bible says, "I know the plans I have for you," but I doubt He was involved in ANY of this nonsense. I did all this stuff on my own, and I'm already feeling like a failure. I keep thinking about the Disney song lyrics of "Let it go! Let it go." The truth is, I don't cook. When I read cookbooks I get a stomach ache. So why am I doing this to myself? I hate crafts and all things crafty. Was there something being pumped in the store air? I gotta get a grip. I have to realize there are things that I'm spectacular at and things I'm not. I can write a manuscript in thirty days. I can speak in front of thousands of people. I can pray for hours with a friend in need and be a battle warrior and answer 120,294,029 e-mails simultaneously. So I can't cook. My kids aren't starving, and if I really want to learn I can try to take some lessons.

I can't be so overwhelmed by my goals that I roll over and don't do any of them. I have to attack them accordingly and remember "nothing is impossible with God." My fear of failure is not healthy. It's time to stop the attitude of "all or nothing." It's dangerous to try and be instantly perfect and then feel defeated. It's not too late for me to cook nice meals for my family. I just might need some help from the frozen foods section at times, and I have to *be okay* with that.

I think God taught me a lesson today from my six-year-old. I said, "Lucy, do you think I'm a good mommy?" She said, "The Best!"

I said, "Why?"

She said, "Just because you're you and that's who God picked out for me! You want to hear a song?" Then she starts to sing these lyrics:

Let It Go

Can't hold it back anymore
Let it go, let it go
Turn away and slam the door
I don't care what they're going to say
It's funny how some distance
Makes everything seems small
And the fears that once controlled me
Can't get to me at all
It's time to see what I can do
To test the limits and break through
No right, no wrong, no rules for me,
I'm free.

While Lucy was singing, the most amazing thing happened. My three-year-old started to chime in with her sister. I've never heard Ruby sing actual lyrics before, but today was the day she started. She's been a slow talker and I prayed this milestone would come and indeed it happened. She was so free! She was singing "Let it go! Let it go!" An answered prayer was in my kitchen. Who knew God speaks through Disney Princesses?

Take a MOMENT to think about . . .

1. How many resolutions do you make every year? Do you keep them? Are they good for you or bad?

2. Is there any area in your life you need to cut yourself some slack in?

Lord, Help me to be like my kids. They are limitless and they are not bound by time lines and thoughts of defeat. I see their playful spirits soaring. Give me the same freedom they have, God. Help me to sing with my kids today and "Let it go" so I can be closer to you. Amen.

Never Give Up on Your Dreams

They found rich, good pasture, and the land was spacious, peaceful and quiet. ~ 1 Chronicles 4:40 (NIV)

This devotion is not only a lesson in delegating, which allows me to go get that much needed pedicure, but also gives my friend Wendy Hagen a chance to tell you her dreams. What dream, you might ask? To simply sleep in . . . So, off I go to get pretty! Enjoy! ~ Kerri

From Wendy:

My kids are older now, almost ready for college. They should at least be able to get up *quietly* in the morning and feed themselves, right? After all, Jordis is five, Lydia is seven, and Elijah is nine. So at my husband's suggestion, I left this note posted in several noticeable places for our kids to see upon waking up.

Dear Hagen Children,

Good morning. Please let Dad and I sleep in. You may play quietly (no TV) until 8:45 a.m. Do not get out any paint, glitter, or glue. In other words, don't make a big mess. You can eat breakfast. Bowls and cereal choices are on the table. Elijah can help with milk. DO NOT come and ask us for a different breakfast or different cereal.

At 8:45 a.m. you can turn on the TV. If there is any screaming or fighting, you will all lose TV for three days. If you come and wake us up for a NON-emergency, there will be consequences.

If Shiner barks, please let her in or out.

We love you and we love our sleep.

Love,

The Best Mom and Dad Ever

You are probably guessing that my husband and I slept in without interruption until 10 a.m. because dreams really do come true. Well, we were awakened from our dreams at 7:15. (I know some of you are already hating on me because your kids never sleep past 5:30, and for that I'm sorry and God bless you.) The cat was the first to wake us up, moaning and meowing at our door, which mysteriously got shut. Then the dog joined in and started barking.

At some point in the 7:00's the girls woke up and Jordis came in with her first emergency. She was all worked up, "My soccer ball is gone. I can't find it. It's not here. Where is it? (Sob, sob.) I can't find it. (Sob, sob.)" I told her where to find it and she left. For a few minutes. Then she came in hysterical because she wanted milk in her cereal and Lydia couldn't get it for her and Elijah was asleep. And she never, ever, ever, never gets cereal. And she can't eat it without milk (cry, cough, squeal, cough up phlegm, sob, whine, cough up a lung). By now it's 8:15, I think. I take her in the bathroom and put on a steamy shower and sit on the floor with her to try and loosen up her cough/snot. (She had a fever and cough for a few days. And now we were dealing with the residual cough enhanced by the emergency crying.) I told Jordis she would need to have something else for breakfast besides cereal because the milk would just make her cough and snot worse. (Whine, cry, complain, cough.) After the steamer, I told my husband he was on duty and crawled back into bed. But don't you fear, we will try this again soon, my friends. Totally Desperate Moms never give up hope. We just keep our expectations low.

Take a MOMENT to think about . . .

1. What can you do this week to try and get extra sleep? Seriously, sleep is so important. It is really hard to focus on the Lord, let alone be a decent parent when you are tired.

2. Got any snot in your life that needs to be loosened up? Bitterness? Jealousy? Unforgiveness? Resentment? Anger? Hurt feelings? This might sound weird, but sometimes my shower time is my best prayer time so work with me on this: take a long, hot shower at least once this week and ask God to help loosen up the snot in your life.

God, Thank You for warm beds even though most of us moms don't spend nearly enough time in them. Thank You for the blessing of motherhood even though it interrupts our sleep lifestyles. Thank You for the privilege of being able to hold our kids next to the steamy shower to loosen up the snot in their lives. Thank You for allowing us to interrupt You all the time with our "emergencies" while You sit and hold us and help loosen up the snot in our lives. Amen.

Single Girls Speak Out to Moms

"Then they can urge the younger women to love their husbands and children, to be self-controlled and pure, to be busy at home, to be kind, and to be subject to their husbands, so that no one will malign the word of God."
~ Titus 2:4–5 (NIV)

Here are some thoughts from my friend, comedian, and mentee Kristin Weber. I just read this and am appalled at her behavior. But then again the babysitting was FREE! I must admit she does make some valid points.

From Kristin:

When Kerri's daughter, Ruby, was about nine months old, I accidentally dropped her while she was in a stroller taking her for a walk. I can share this now because Ruby is a happy, healthy three-year-old with no evidence of permanent stroller-tipping damage.

Ruby was securely strapped in the buggy when we set out to walk to a nearby coffee shop, hoping to give Kerri a little time for herself to gather whatever sanity having a husband, two kids, and a comedy career had left her. (Believe me, not much. I say that in Christian love and cause she'll probably edit it out of this book anyway.)

As we crossed a street, I didn't see a crack in the cement by the curb, and the stroller hit the bump and tipped completely backward. Ruby stayed securely fastened, thanks to my stellar buckling-in skills, but as I picked the stroller up from its upside down position, Ruby and I locked eyes and shared a mutual thought: *Really? Kerri entrusted me with you? Really?*

This brings us to a somewhat delicate topic that often gets overlooked in the sphere of church: doing life with people who aren't in your life stage. When you get married, your priorities change. They change even more when you have kids. You can't go gallivanting last minute to a movie, and even a simple errand can take reinforcements.

As a single person, I haven't lived it, but I get it. But that's not a reason to drop your single friends once you say

"I do." You need, perhaps more importantly than before, to keep them in your life.

Why? Because of the "Titus 2 effect." We single ladies need to be mentored by you married folk. We need to see the good and the bad. So just realize that we are here for each other. You help us see the joy and excitement that comes with having a loving home. And you get free baby-sitting on occasions. Yes, we might end up injuring your child, but isn't that free hour worth it in the end?

Take a MOMENT to think about . . .

1. Do you have any single friends that you can mentor and encourage while they are still single?
2. How can you get help from others without being a burden to them? What kind of trade-off is possible?

Dear Lord, Thank You for all types of friendships. Thank You for always giving me the support I need, through Yourself and through others. You have blessed me greatly and for that I am so thankful. Amen.

Best Shabbat Ever

*"Start children off on the way they should go,
and even when they are old they will not turn from it."*
~ Proverbs 22:6 *(NIV)*

I've always been a big believer of kids being exposed to different cultures and even religions. Being a good Christian girl growing up, I had a ministry for cute single Jewish men. It was called JFK, Jews for Kerri. My slogans were: "We only need one!" "Try the ham! The food's better on our team!" "Try my Bible but keep reading after Malachi . . . it gets better." I had all kinds of slogans. So why Jewish men? (1) They love their mothers. (2) They are usually very witty. (3) They have 401 K plans! So yes I drove my mother crazy by dating all the "wrong" guys and my Jewish boyfriends' mothers weren't exactly thrilled to meet me either. When I got engaged, one of my ex's Jewish mothers wanted to send me a gift.

So of course I wasn't surprised for Lucy to have a Jewish boyfriend from the time she was two. David and Lucy played together and his mother and I have planned their wedding just like *Fiddler on the Roof*. We've always told Lucy to be an evangelist so many a time in a car ride I'd overhear her, "David, do you have Jesus in your heart? You know you need Jesus." David would say, "Who?" I'd yell from the front seat, "Ask your mother!" Yaira and I kid about our interfaith couple all the time, and she's actually an amazing friend and strong prayer warrior for me. I think she prays better than half my Christian friends. It's not uncommon for her to say, "The Devil is a liar, remember that Kerri!"

We were invited last Friday to a traditional Jewish Shabbat Dinner at Yaira and her husband Jeff's home with their sons. We were excited to teach Lucy all the traditions. She of course was excited to eat like the Israelites did as she put it. She also wore a long dress in honor of Queen Esther who was her favorite Jewish heroine. So we get there and find out about some special candle lighting ceremony. Both my girls want to wear yamakas. I'm not sure it's Kosher but they were allowed.

So we sat at the table after some beautiful Jewish prayers, blessings, and chanting. It was all very orderly and respectful and even solemn in a good way. Everything was lovely. Lucy didn't say anything for five whole minutes. She clinked her glass and loudly said, "Everyone, I'd like to say something! Pleeeeeease!" So we quieted down for Miss Lucy to speak and she raised her grape juice glass and said in these exact words. "In the New Testament when Jesus came, He said take this bread. It is My body. Eat of it in remembrance of Me. Take this cup, it is My blood. Drink it in remembrance of Me." Lucy recited the entire communion service without stopping. There was at first an awkward silence, then stares of embarrassment (Kerri and Ron), amazement (Jeff and Yaira), and confusion (their boys). People tried to interrupt her but she wasn't having it. I heard the boys say, "Dad, who is she talking about?" I looked over at Jeff across the table and said, "BEST Shabbat ever! Right?" He just laughed and Lucy's sermon concluded. She was one step away from an alter call.

My little evangelist. I didn't know what to make of her behavior. In essence, wasn't she just being true to the person we raised her to be? Wasn't she doing as Jesus commanded her . . . to go and make disciples of all men? I was the one with the "issues," not wanting to offend our hosts. I think I learned I need to more like my daughter. She's bold in her faith. She's unafraid of what other people think because she believes in her heart that any event about the Bible should include her perspective about Jesus, her Lord and Savior. I have to say, all in all I'm pretty proud of my kid. She marches to her own drummer. But then again so did Jesus and all of His crew. I must be doing something right.

Take a MOMENT to think about . . .

1. Have you raised your kids to publicly share about their faith? If so, are they doing it? If not, would you be willing to talk to them about it now?

2. Does that scare you to talk about your faith journey with friends from different back grounds? How can you overcome your fear?

Dear God, Thank You for my children that know more about speaking the truth than I do sometimes. Thank You for the gift of bold faith that You've given them. Help me to be more like them. Use me to continue to guide my kids in walking with You all the days of their lives. Amen.

Clutter, Clutter, Clutter

"Two are better than one, because they have a good return for their labor: If either of them falls down, one can help the other up." ~ Ecclesiastes 4:9–10 (NIV)

My friend Claire Lee and I have been friends since our kids were six months old. We have play dates while we work on movie scripts and plan our next European vacation when we hit it big. We had our first daughters together, our second as well. One day she shared she was prego with her third. I laughed out loud! Okay, not the most supportive response, but that was when I knew I was "done" having kids. Between the two of us, she clearly has more clutter in her home than I. It's all her fault because she had to go and have that "third kid!" Below are her thoughts on a mother's clutter:

From Claire Lee:

My life is full of clutter. Everywhere I look, it's all I see. Toys here, clothes there, shoes . . . wait, where are the shoes? I only see one! Everything is everywhere you look, but never there when you really need it. My son loves to hide things—remotes, bills, his shoes. I'm constantly picking up after everyone and then as soon as I do, they make a mess again. Sigh. I knew motherhood would be a handful, I just didn't realize how exhausting it would be to cook, clean, deal with gross bodily excrements, chauffeur kids, get groceries, clean, pick up kids, take kids to classes, clean, cook, then clean again. Sometimes I miss having a job to go to so I can talk to adults! And not CLEAN!

When they say, "It takes a village," they really do mean it takes an entire village. I have a husband, parents, and an arsenal of friends that I rely on to help me raise my kids. I don't know how a single mother does it. They're amazing. My son will often run and hug my friends before he hugs me . . . Uh, so not cool, buddy! But that's how I know how much my kids love the people in their lives.

By the way, it wasn't always this way. In the beginning I thought I had to do it on my own, because how can I be a stay-at-home mom and have people helping me? If this is my purpose, shouldn't I be able to do it without burdening someone else? But God says in Ecclesiastes 4:9–10, "Two are better than one, because they have a good return for their labor: If either of them falls down, one can help the other up." And believe me, I've fallen flat on my face many times, and luckily I've had people to pick me up.

Something that took me a while to learn is how to ask for help and how to receive. So when someone offers to babysit, bring me a meal, or to drive my kids' home, I've learned it's okay to just say, "Thank you." Because God knows I need that manicure, nap, or just a little breathing room so I don't go crazy and lock myself in the pantry to eat chocolate. (Yes, I've done it, please don't judge.)

It takes strength to be vulnerable and ask for help. And by receiving, it lightens the burden and deepens friendships, allowing others to pour out God's blessings. Just one small thing can make a huge impact in my day and help make the clutter a little more manageable.

Take a MOMENT to think about . . .

1. Are you good at asking for help or are you trying to do it all?

2. Is there an area in your life you could use a little hand in? Pray to God to send some help your way.

Dear God, Thank You for bringing friends into our lives to help us on the journey. Please send me whoever You want to be on my support team as I endeavor to survive the next "child rearing years" of my life. Help me to ask for help when I need it and be grateful when it's offered. Amen.

So This Is the End (until my next book)

Yes, my friends, we've come to the end of our journey. For some of you it's taken months to get through this book, "one potty sitting" at a time. For some of you, you have read the whole thing at the bank while sitting in line. I know what you're thinking, "What? This is the end? But whatever happens to this crazy woman? Did her kids survive preschool or did Child Protective Services finally crack down on her? Did she ever figure out how to cook? Did she ever find inner peace?"

And I'm asking myself the question, "What did my readers learn from me, bearing my soul and other body parts to them in this book. What was the point of this book and me writing it?" Well in short, I hope you lost a few things and gained some others. Such as:

1. You lost a few pounds from laughing at my dysfunction (key word FUN).

2. You lost some judgment of yourself as a mother and realized you're not the only one who makes cereal a dinner entrée and watches too much reality TV.

3. You no longer compare yourself with other moms and how you're doing on the scale of one to Mary Poppins.

4. You've lost the feeling that you are alone with all your "issues" and questions as we travel through the motherhood jungle together. You are NEVER alone! God always has your back and now you realize so do I. I will always be more messed up than you. Count on it!

5. You've realized that you have a second, third and even a forty-sixth chance when it comes to starting over with our kids. You now know that it is never too late to try to love them like Jesus would.

Some things I hope you've gained:

1. You've gained the knowledge that you are a ROCKSTAR person. You matter to God and this world, outside of your child-rearing capabilities. You're a daughter of the King of the universe. Get out your tiara and dance! (Preferably to some praise music or 80s song . . . could be the same thing!)

2. You've gained a different way to look at icky, messy, even hurtful situations knowing that they are not permanent and good things will come. You have gained God's perspective that He's not crying over spilt milk shakes and neither should you.

3. You've gained the knowledge that God was a Parent and He gave His only Baby for you to die on that cross so you don't have to carry all your sins. He is the best Parent in the world and wants to take it off your back . . . you just have to let Him.

4. You've gained the knowledge that we are never going to know it all, have it all, or control it all. So we can stop trying and realize that we need to take our hands off the control panel every single day and give it up to the One who's really driving . . . our God.

5. You've gained a way to laugh at yourself and the crazy, hilarious high-speed freeway called Motherhood, knowing full well that there are no exits. Know that motherhood, parenting, never ends, so we might as well laugh our heads off, get some popcorn (insert your favorite food here), and enjoy the ride. God has a sense of humor. He created YOUR KIDS!

I hope you've had as much fun as I have walking with me through these adventures. It scares and excites me as I sit here writing my goodbye for now, knowing that so many of you know soooo much about me and all my struggles and issues (prayer requests). I feel like we're friends. You know you can find me on Facebook (Kerri Pomarolli) or my website www.kerripom.com. I'd love to hear from you. I hope this starts a trend of more of us getting "real" for real. We're not fooling as many as we think anyway. Remember that we have the most important job on Earth, we're mothers. As my good friend Willie Wonka said, "We are the music makers. We are the dreamers of dreams." Don't ever stop dreaming. Don't ever stop believing in those dreams, because those dreams become reality when you teach your children. Nothing is impossible with God and a mother who loves them.

So I'll leave you with this quote from Pablo Picasso: "My mother said to me, 'If you are a soldier, you will be general. If you are a monk, you will become pope. Instead I was a painter and I became a painter and I became Picasso.'"